Coley Talking

Margaret Ounsley has lived in Coley for 35 years. Having completed an MSc in English Local History at the University of Oxford, she is currently pursuing doctoral research on Reading's Elizabethan Poor Law at the University of Reading. She worked on the original Coley Oral History project in 1989, with other members of the Coley Local History Group. Her fascination with this very special and absorbing neighbourhood continues.

Also published by Two Rivers Press

When Reading Really Rocked by Adrian Moulton, Mike Warth & Austin Matthews
Bricks & Brickwork in Reading: Patterns & Polychromy by Adam Sowan
Reading's Influential Women by Terry Dixon & Linda Saul
The Whole Story: Painting more than just the flowers by Christina Hart-Davies
The Art and History of Whiteknights edited by Jenny Halstead
The Art of Peter Hay by John Froy with Martin Andrews
Signs of the Times: Reading's Memorials by Malcolm Summers
Rural Reading by Adrian Lawson & Geoff Sawers
The Constitutionals: A work of fiction by Peter Robinson
Botanical Artistry: Plants, projects & processes by Julia Trickey
The Greenwood Trees: History, folklore and uses of Britain's trees by Christina Hart-Davies
Reading Abbey and the Abbey Quarter by Peter Durrant & John Painter
Reading's Bayeux Tapestry by Reading Museum
A Coming of Age: Celebrating 18 Years of Botanical Painting by the Eden Project Florilegium Society by Ros Franklin
Picture Palace to Penny Plunge: Reading's Cinemas by David Cliffe
The Shady Side of Town: Reading's Trees by Adrian Lawson & Geoff Sawers
Reading: The Place of the People of the Red One by Duncan Mackay
Silchester: Life on the Dig by Jenny Halstead & Michael Fulford
The Writing on the Wall by Peter Kruschwitz
Caught on Camera: Reading in the 70s by Terry Allsop
Plant Portraits by Post: Post & Go British Flora by Julia Trickey
Allen W. Seaby: Art and Nature by Martin Andrews & Robert Gillmor
Reading Detectives by Kerry Renshaw
Fox Talbot & the Reading Establishment by Martin Andrews
All Change at Reading by Adam Sowan
Cover Birds by Robert Gillmor
Caversham Court Gardens: A Heritage Guide by Friends of Caversham Court Gardens
Birds, Blocks & Stamps: Post & Go Birds of Britain by Robert Gillmor
Down by the River: The Thames and Kennet in Reading by Gillian Clark

Coley Talking

Realities of life in old Reading

Margaret Ounsley

First published in the UK in 2021 by Two Rivers Press
7 Denmark Road, Reading RG1 5PA
www.tworiverspress.com

© Two Rivers Press 2021
© in text Margaret Ounsley
© in pictures, see picture credits

The right of the author to be identified as the author of the work has been asserted by her in accordance with the Copyright, Designs and Patents Act of 1988.

All rights reserved. No part of this publication may be reproduced, stored in or introduced into a retrieval system, or transmitted, in any form, or by any means (electronic, mechanical, photocopying, recording or otherwise) without the prior written permission of the publisher.

ISBN 978-1-909747-88-3

1 2 3 4 5 6 7 8 9

Two Rivers Press is represented in the UK by Inpress Ltd and distributed by Ingram Publisher Services UK.

'Coley Steps' © Reading Museum (Reading Borough Council)
Text and cover design by Nadja Guggi and typeset in Parisine

Printed and bound in Great Britain by Ashford Colour Press, Gosport

Acknowledgements

1989
The original interviewees were: Mr Adey, Mr Absolom, Mr Akeby, Mr Allwood, Mr Atkinson, Mrs Beach, Mr Beats, Mr R. Booth, Mrs K. Coggins, Mrs Curtis, Mr W. Denton, Mrs D. Flatman, Mr Fuller, Mr C. Gorse, Mr Gutteridge, Mr Hathaway, Mrs E. Ilsley, Mr E. Kendal, Mr. B Milham, Mrs I. Milham, Mrs E. Neal, Mrs H. Noakes, Mrs Rayburn, Mr R. Robertts, Mrs J. Sherriff, Mrs H. Stokes, Mrs L. Taylor, Mr Turner, Mr C. Wells, Mr White.

Further contributions were from: Mr B. Elam, Mr D. Noyes.

The interviewers were: Mr D. Noyes, Ms M. Ounsley, Mrs B. Parry, Mr I. Parry, Ms M. Panetta, Ms F. Stradling.

Background research was carried out by: Ms M. Ounsley, Ms M. Panetta

Text: Ms M. Ounsley

Our thanks go to: Margaret Smith and the Local Studies Department of Reading Library for their help; Peter Durrant and the staff of the Berkshire Record Office for their help and guidance; John Rhodes and Sue Read and Reading Museum for copying photographs; Brigit Hutter for interview advice; Barbara Hurst of Coley Primary School for access to the logbooks; The University of Reading's Photographic Services, Departments of Geography and Typography and Graphic Communication; Tammy Bedford and the community grants service of Reading Borough Council for making it all possible.

Further acknowledgements 2020
Despite the restrictions of the COVID-19 lockdown the staff of the Berkshire Record Office have been as helpful as ever.

Thanks also to Joe Doak and Graham Turner, moderators of the History and Events of Coley Reading Facebook group, for their help and advice.

The author's royalties are to be donated to Coley Primary School.

Picture credits

- p. xii Map of Old Coley © Sally Castle
- p. xiv 1643 map; from Guilding, *Diary of the Corporation of Reading* (Parker and Co) 1892. Photo by Robert Ounsley
- p. 2 Buck's View of Reading, 1734. Courtesy of the illustrations collection, Reading Central Library
- p. 4 James Elisha. By permission of Richard Lofthouse
- p. 17 Coley School plans. Photo by Joe Doak by permission of Sarah Pengelly, Coley Primary
- p. 18 Coley School today. Photo by Robert Ounsley
- p. 22 St Saviours Church. Photo by Robert Ounsley
- p. 26 OS map, 1900. Reproduced under a Creative Commons Attribution-NonCommercial-ShareAlike 4.0 International Public License (CC-BY-NC-SA) with the permission of the National Library of Scotland
- p. 28 Coley Goods Station. By permission of Graham Turner
- p. 32 Coley Steps © Reading Museum (Reading Borough Council). All rights reserved
- p. 36 Slums. Courtesy of Berkshire Record Office (D/EX1722/14/1)
- p. 46 Old British School today. Photo by Robert Ounsley
- p. 55 Shop. By permission of Graham Holt
- p. 56 Fish & chip shop. By permission of Nigel Richards
- p. 58 Bristows. By permission of Jenny & John Ballard
- p. 60 Blue Lion. By permission of Ron Comley
- p. 61 Blue Lion crowd. By permission of Ron Comley
- p. 62 The Borough Arms. By permission of Raymond Simonds
- p. 70 Infants © Reading Museum (Reading Borough Council). All rights reserved
- p. 90 VE Day, Garnet Street © Reading Museum (Reading Borough Council). All rights reserved
- p. 91 Coley Street with girls in foreground. By permission of Mary O'Sullivan
- p. 93 Castle Tap. Photo by Robert Ounsley
- p. 94 Field Road subsidence © Reading Museum (Reading Borough Council). All rights reserved

*For the children of Coley,
past, present and future*

Contents

Notes | x

I. Pigney's Lane | 1
II. Talking of living conditions | 29
III. Talking of making ends meet | 42
IV. Talking of the Coley community | 55
V. Talking of growing up in Coley | 69
VI. Talking of health, medicine, illness and death | 80
VII. Coley moves on | 88
Postscript: Old Coley now | 93

Endnotes | 96
Bibliography | 99

Notes

History of the project

In 1989 the Coley Local History Group began an oral history project of the area known as 'Old Coley', in particular of the northern part known as the 'Steps' and its surrounding courts and passages. Residents and ex-residents, many quite elderly, were interviewed for their memories of a way of life long gone. The results were published in two little books, *Talking of Coley* and *More Talking of Coley*. Thirty years on, interest in the area is still as great, but the little books have become tattered or hard to find. This reissue combines the two publications, with added chapters on how Old Coley first developed and on the later clearances and redevelopment that was eventually to disperse a whole community.

Chapters II.–VI. are from the original publications and have 'Talking of' incorporated into their chapter headings to differentiate the old material from the new. The original text has been edited slightly to streamline the content and correct one or two factual errors.

Location

Old Coley is the area south of Castle Hill, east of Coley Avenue, north of Berkeley Avenue and west of the Kennet. You would be able to see virtually all that remains of it today by standing on the footbridge that goes over the Inner Distribution Road (IDR) by the Salvation Army hostel. A school, a few streets of terraced houses, and a church. There are few indications of the extensive community that once lived in the dense, packed streets and courts under the IDR and up the hill. Other buildings further up the Kennet, and Rifle Range Cottages and Coley Kiln Cottages, have also been included in this study whereas the area around Coley Hill has not.

Local names

Locally Coley Passage was known as the 'Steps' because it was built up the side of a hill, the houses rising in tiers up the hillside. Garnet Hill was known as Stoney Hill simply because it was! At its top Dover

Street met Coley Place and – perhaps to separate the newer, better housing from the worse – a brick wall divided the two streets. As is the nature of things this was soon breached, and for many years the wall stood with a large arch in it called 'The hole in the wall'. Eventually the wall itself disappeared.

OLD COLEY

1. Bricklayers Arms
2. Rose & Crown
3. The Borough Arms
4. Brickmakers
5. The Blue Lion

This map of Old Coley, designed and illustrated by Sally Castle, shows some of the places and people mentioned in this book, and the location of the Inner Distribution Road (IDR) in Reading today.

The construction of the IDR in the 1960s involved the bulldozing of Coley Street, and the last pubs and shops it contained, as well as the removal of Henrietta Street, Bright Street and Parnell Street.

The numbered beer mugs represent some of these public houses; other pubs included the Spotted Cow and the Coachmakers Arms on Coley Street, the Hit and Miss, and the Wooden Walls of England just off Coley Steps and three more at the top in Coley Place: the John Bull, the Crown and the Bricklayers.

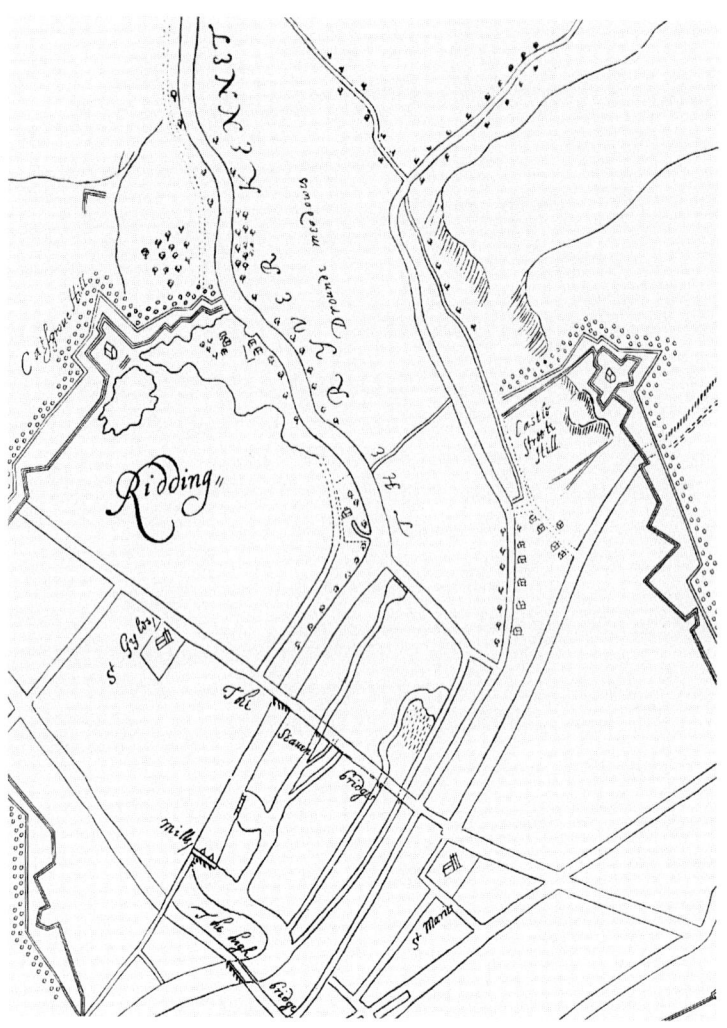

Map of Civil War defences, 1643, showing Pigney's Lane. The map is oriented to the west, with St Mary's Minster at the bottom and Castle Hill going up to the defences, roughly where Field Road is today. Pigney's Lane is shown as a row of houses, with some more along the Holybrook.

I. Pigney's Lane

The growth and development of Coley, its life, people and institutions, 1700–1900

Early beginnings

In 1643, at the height of the Civil War, Parliamentary troops laid siege to Reading, and defences were built around its western edge by the King's men, encamped in the town. A sketch of those defences was drawn up and remains in the Corporation records. It shows Coley as a lane from Castle Street down to the Holybrook, a few houses strung along it and the brook itself. This is the earliest map we have showing any community in Coley.[1]

This lane was known as Pigney's Lane certainly by the 1640s, when Baptists were recorded as meeting there. It was convenient for them to make their escape across the Holybrook when raided.[2] It is likely that the name is older than that.

Place name origins often involve guesswork, but the word 'piggesnye', literally 'pig's eye', meant a sweetheart, or darling. Chaucer says of Alison in *The Miller's Tale* that 'She was a ... piggesnye for any lord to leggen in his bed'.[3] It would not be too much of a stretch to consider that this poor little outcrop of Reading was, in its origins, the haunt of prostitutes and the semi-criminal. As the 18th century proceeded the name was more often written as Pickney or Pinckney, perhaps in an attempt at decorousness. Grape Passage, directly opposite on Castle Street, appears as 'Grope Passage' in earlier documents, renamed for perhaps the same reasons.[4]

This area was part of the much larger Coley Park Estate, which stretched between Southcote and Whitley and had been owned by the Vachell family since the early 14th century. This little section of the estate seems to have been regarded separately from the fields, water meadows, orchards and gardens of the rest of the estate. Deeds from 1653 refer to it as 'Coley Parva' or Little Coley.[5]

The Thompson family, who owned the estate from 1727, parcelled up and mortgaged the area to raise money in 1734, when it was described as:

All that Mead or Meadow Ground commonly called or known by the name of Pinckneys or Pickneys or by whatsoever other name the same that was or had been called or known.[6]

An engraving from that same year gives a view of Coley from the south and east from Katesgrove. It shows the Kennet and behind it the Holybrook, with flat, tilled grounds, almost certainly the bleaching grounds referred to in later maps, where cloth was laid out to bleach in the sun. We see a few houses strung along a lane, and, at the top of Castle Hill, the King's Arms public house, which still exists as a private house. A document from 1748 describes the buildings around Pigney's Lane as 'workshops, warehouses, edifices and buildings' as well as tenements.[7] This conjures a hotch-potch of activity and mixed development, typical of the time.

In 1783 the clerk of St Mary's parish took a census of households, giving us the first named residents of Coley. It lists 24 households on the eastern and western sides of Pigney's Lane, which the parish clerk estimated as representing about 125 people.[8] These people

1734 View of Reading, showing Coley. The artist would have been standing where the modern Alpine Street in Katesgrove is.

were the 'undertenants' of a Mr James Smith, who himself leased the land from William Chamberlayne, owner of Coley Park. In March 1802 Chamberlayne's son sold the estate to a Thomas Bradford of Sussex for £30,960.

Thomas Bradford was a wealthy landowner and probably saw the estate as a good investment. It is not clear that he ever lived there. Just a month after acquiring the estate, in April 1802, he sold most of the Pigney's Lane area to Francis Lovelock and Thomas Tanner, who owned Little Coley Farm.[9] The whole estate was then sold later that year to John McDonnell.

It is easy to see why the land around Pigney's Lane was more valuable for development than as bleaching grounds and meadow. In 1740 the population of Reading was estimated at 7,500; in 1801 it was 9,742 and by 1831 it was 15,595. This population explosion in the early years of the century was extraordinary for a market town in the south east of England and well above the national average.[10] St Mary's parish in particular grew, more than doubling its population from 3,156 to 6,798 in the thirty years 1801–1831.[11]

This population boom was fuelled by in-migration. The end of the 18th century saw considerable agricultural distress in Berkshire and surrounding counties and Reading offered jobs in brick-making, brewing, malting, on the canals and in the inns as well as in sail-making and silk-weaving. This, alongside an increase in the marriage rate, drove Reading's growth.[12] A housing boom followed. The number of houses in St Mary's nearly trebled, from 596 to 1,414, over the same period. Coates' map of 1802 shows this area of Coley just as it was sold off and about to be developed.

At this time there was little local authority planning and building control and the quality of developments very much depended on the attitude of the landowner who sold the land. A careful and well-resourced landowner would offer land leasehold, invest in infrastructure and set out minimum standards for building, seeing developments as a long-term investment.[13] As we have seen, Thomas Bradford retained Coley Park Estate for under a year, selling off parts of it, before selling the rest of it on – an asset-stripper in modern terms. The Pigney's Lane land was offered freehold for maximum up-front profit.

Thomas Tanner, who rented Little Coley Farm, and was described as a 'gentleman' in the 1826 pollbook, bought his land for £2,615

James Elisha, one of the early developers of Coley.

in April 1802. Having built Coley Place, Tanner sold on the land in 1809 to a consortium of three builders and others.[14] James Elisha, a builder from Coley Hill, bought nearly half and was responsible for approximately 96 dwellings, including Grape Cottages and Commercial Hall. One of the last developments was in 1836 by a Philip Rose, described as a 'victualler' in 1826 – a pub landlord. He built Rose's Court, to the west of Coley Place.[16]

The number of developers is reflected in the different types of development. About a third of the housing is on a 'courtyard' pattern, including Bosier Square, Marshall Place and Commercial Hall. These normally had an entry at one end and communal facilities such as water taps and closets in the middle or to one side. Others were back-to-back, where a row of terraced houses would share a back wall with houses on the other side, allowing no through ventilation. Some, such as Hanover Square, were courtyard *and* back-to-back.[17]

By the end of this building boom Coley had been reshaped. The pollbook of 1826 and a tithe map of 1839 still refer to Pigney's Lane, while the 1837 pollbook and 1841 census have the renamed Coley Street. However, newspaper articles refer to 'Pigney-lane' as late as 1843, so it stuck for many years as a local name. The 1841 census shows nearly all of this part of Coley in place with a population of 1,018.[18]

Similar developments occurred elsewhere, in places such as Silver Street and Hosier Street. The impact on the sanitation and public health of the town was soon apparent. A cholera epidemic in 1830 led to the establishment of a Board of Health (soon disbanded). A typhus epidemic, which swept Reading in 1846, stimulated an inquiry into sanitary conditions in the borough. The link between poor housing conditions and public health was well known by this time. However, the local authority simply did not have the power, access to finance and political will to tackle the problem. It was not until 1868 and the Artisans Dwellings Act that local authorities could compel owners to keep their houses in a sanitary condition. Union Square, on the east side of Coley Street, was built sometime after 1867 when St Mary's Workhouse closed, and must be one of the last examples of 'court' housing in Reading, already associated with poor sanitation and ventilation.

In 1881 the Reading Corporation Act finally gave the Corporation the power to block court buildings and insist on a minimum level of sanitation, light and ventilation in new dwellings. In 1888 a series of by-laws set down strict rules for foundations, walls, ventilation, water closets, drainage and minimum space.

Meanwhile, other parts of Coley developed along much improved lines. In 1852 John Bligh Monck, of the Monck family that now owned the estate, leased land adjacent to the Holybrook which was to become Willow Street and Brook Street.[19] Little Coley Farm, predominantly dairy through the most part of the 19th century, providing milk, cream and butter to the town, was turned over to housing sometime before 1887. On this land was built what were to become Wolseley Street, Field Road, Dover Street and Garnet Street. In contrast to Bradford's asset-stripping freehold sale, Bligh Monck maintained the lease, and an interest in housing with basic standards.

We get a little snapshot of this development from Rev. Crawfurd of St Mary's Minster, when he writes of the opening of St Saviour's church in 1887. He walked in procession down Wolseley Street to the new church accompanied by John Bligh Monck:

> He was not a man to be impressed by the ceremonial of the Church and he chatted pleasantly all the way on the changed character of the Coley district as he had known it formerly as meadow land on his estate; and at one spot he led me off out from the procession to show me the site on which Little Coley Farm had formerly been and was now covered with cottages.[20]

In 1875 John Bligh Monck developed further land off Castle Street, between the Holybrook and the Kennet 'well-suited for the Erection of Good Cottages being in the immediate neighbourhood of the Reading Iron Works'.[21] These were to become Henrietta Street, Bright Street, and Parnell Street. The Moncks continued to derive income from these developments until the estate was sold in 1937.[22]

By the 1880s Reading Corporation had the powers to pull down slum housing, yet the Coley slums remained, despite their well-known insanitary conditions. John Shea, Medical Officer of Health, was in a difficult position. Compel landlords to improve their properties, and they put up rents. Condemn properties for clearance and the poor were left with nowhere to go:

I have therefore been careful so far only to condemn houses that were so bad that it was more to the interest of the owner to pull them down than to attempt to repair them.[23]

The 1890 Housing of the Working Classes Act gave local authorities the powers to carry out house building, but across the country these were rarely taken up. Slow progress was made up to 1914 and was further held up by the First World War.

Thus, at the opening of the 20th century the dense, packed streets, courts and passages of Coley that housed our interviewees remained intact.

Living conditions

Throughout the 19th century the conditions in Coley were the subject of reports, inquiries and newspaper coverage, leaving us with a clear picture of what daily life must have been like for its citizens. Our interviewees remembered harsh conditions, but for their Victorian predecessors things were even worse.

The housing was marked out as inadequate from its very beginning. Rev. Sherman, writing in 1850, recalled the conditions when he arrived as a curate to St Mary's Castle Street in 1835:

> In all towns there is usually a special locality where the poorest and most wretched of the inhabitants dwell. This locality in Reading was Hanover-Square in Coley-lane ... its houses were very filthy, and its residents the worst of the population of that otherwise clean and respectable town.[24]

In contrast to Sherman's 'clean and respectable town' the inquiry instigated by the Corporation after the typhoid epidemic in 1846, managed by John Billing, revealed insanitary conditions across the town: 95 per cent of properties had no drainage of any kind, most used cesspits, while 387 houses drained directly into the Kennet. A resident of Reading could expect to die five years earlier than nearby Wokingham or Easthampstead.[25]

A government commission followed, which heard evidence from the 2 February to the 9 March 1847. One witness was Thomas Harman, who in 1841 was living in Hanover Square. The *Reading Mercury* reports that he stated that 14 families resided there, comprising about 40 persons, and there was only one spring for the use of *all* of them. There was a well situated within six yards of the cesspool, and the water was so much tainted with the effluvia from it, that they could not use it, consequently they were obliged to go to the Holy Brook, a distance of about 400 yards.[26]

A private bill to deal with the issues failed after opposition from ratepayers and the *Reading Mercury*. The 1848 Public Health Act left too much to local authorities' discretion, and in Reading was ineffective. A permanent Board of Health was established, with an Inspector of Nuisances, who reported regularly on the problems in Coley, as elsewhere. However, most of the properties were owned by small landlords (some living in the same streets) with precious little resource themselves, and the authority had no powers to oblige them to deal with insanitary conditions.

In 1865 the Inspector reported about Martha Place:

> the privies is intolerable, many of them close to the back doors and full to overflowing...the manure boiling through the floor and lying in large quantities. The whole of the houses in Martha Place is the property of John Newman, No. 1 Martha Place. I saw Mrs Newman, who seemed to think it quite a hardship to be obliged to have the privies emptied.[27]

A Board of Health inspection of both Bosier Square and Castle Hill Place in 1870 considered them to be unfit for human habitation if immediate remedial work was not done, while the wells supplying water to Fir Court and Martha Place were 'impure'.[28]

A proper drainage system was implemented across the town through the 1870s, so that by 1885 John Shea, Medical Officer of Health, was able to report that the abolition of cesspools in the borough was approaching completion, with less than 400 houses left to connect.[29] By 1900 even Coley had mains drainage and standpipes with fresh water supplied to the streets and courts, although these were shared.

However, while diseases associated with poor sanitation, such as cholera and typhoid, were on the wane, those associated with overcrowding and poor living conditions, such as tuberculosis and typhus, remained. Ironically the enlightened Forster's Education Act of 1870 actually provided a new vector for the spread of childhood diseases such as measles, whooping cough and scarlet fever. These swept through the poorer areas on a seasonal basis, with fatal consequences. John Shea noted that deaths were mostly 'among the children of the poor',[30] and many schools closed to prevent disease spreading.

The first easily available systematic count of childhood and infant mortality is in the 1911 census when women in households were asked how many live births they had had, and how many children were still alive. If we take the 24 households of Bosier Square as an example, a total of 28 children died in 9 households over the preceding years. These were all live births, and any number of weeks, months or years old. Measles, mumps, whooping cough and diarrhoea were the great killers, the latter often caused by feeding with dirty bottles, in the opinion of the Medical Officer of Health in 1902, Dr Ashby.[31] Most research indicates, however, that working class women breastfed their babies to a greater extent than the middle class did at this time, so he may have been extrapolating from the wider population.[32]

Population and employment

Despite high infant mortality, the 19th century population of Coley would have seemed very young to us. The 1841 census reveals more than 50 per cent of the population below the age of 20, while only 12 inhabitants were over 70. This profile changes little into the 20th century. In 1911 in Bosier Square, of the 104 souls crammed in, 37 were children under 14, and 18 were age 6 and under. The noises of crying and playing children would have been a constant background, which we in our increasingly aging society have almost forgotten. In contrast there were only five adults over 65.

Adults were largely unskilled workers. Censuses before 1841 give little detail, but by looking at the fathers' occupations in baptismal records for 1813–1819 on Pigney's Lane the vast majority are 'labourers' with the occasional soldier or bargeman listed. By the 1841 census 355 people were recorded as working, the most popular occupations in Coley being labourer, silk weaver, shoe maker, and agricultural labourer.

'Labourer' covered any number of unskilled and casual jobs that would normally be picked up for a day rate, such as unloading carts, moving earth or shifting lumber. As soon as a person had permanent employ in a trade, they were much more likely to describe themselves more specifically as a 'brewer's servant' or 'sawyer' for example. It is clear that by far the biggest trade was silk-weaving, with ancillary silk occupations, such as 'throwster' or 'twister'.

Reading did not have the large silk spinning and weaving factories found in northern cities such as Derby and Macclesfield.[33] Instead, at the beginning of the 19th century it operated a form of sweatshop labour called 'half-apprenticeship'. Young adolescents would be taken on without indentures, thus with none of the normal protections, paid a low rate, and laid off when their term was finished, unless they could pay an entry fine, which few could. Typically, they were housed in small workshops of nine or ten semi-skilled workers under the supervision of one skilled man.[34] The 1826 pollbook names[15] silk manufacturers or processors who were sufficiently wealthy to vote, one of whom, Thomas Gutteridge, lived in Coley Terrace. An 1818 parliamentary inquiry heard that most silk weavers in Reading lived in St Mary's parish, and were either being thrown 'on the parish' or into prostitution when their time was up.[35] John Berkeley Monck, owner of the Coley Park Estate from 1809, had intervened to warn young people against taking jobs in the industry.

The industry was particularly vulnerable to economic downturns as well as changes in fashion, and in 1829 260 silk weavers were reported unemployed across the town, which would have disproportionately affected Coley. John Berkeley Monck was one of the first to contribute to a collection to buy them bread.[36]

By 1841 the large silk-weaving factory of Baylis and Co. Crape Manufacturers opened on the edge of the Kennet by the Kings Road. Crape manufacturing was predominantly done on the large power loom, and in conditions little better than the sweatshops, with young, mostly female underpaid labour. One of these was Sarah Parsons, 15, of Box Court, Coley who in August 1842 was dragged into the open machinery and killed.[37] Nonetheless the Reading industry simply could not compete with the larger northern factories.

There were a number of brick kilns in and around Coley in 1841, one, Castle Kiln, was at the corner of what is now Garnet Hill; another, Avenue Kiln nearer to modern Boston Avenue; and Coley Kiln stood where the current St Saviour's church is. Despite this, only a handful name a related occupation in the 1841 census – three brickmakers, two potters and six bricklayers. It is possible that casual labour accounted for this, but it is noticeable there were more shoemakers and agricultural labourers than brickmakers.

By 1871 this situation had changed considerably. The census shows approximately one third of adult males working in brick- or pottery-related jobs, such as brickmaker's labourers or bricklayers. The returns do not show the extent of the child labour in the kilns, but this was evident to teachers in the first 'Ragged School' who noticed that, after a day's work in the kilns children came to the evening class 'with hands so stiffened and often clogged with clay, that they were ... little fitted to use a pen'.[38] Silk weaving had disappeared completely by this time.

By 1891 brickmaking had been replaced by jobs at the biscuit factory and the iron works, as well as shop work and domestic service. Despite the changes in industry the working people of Coley always fell into that 'unskilled labour' category – the most vulnerable to downturns and the most lacking in protection. A 1912 study of poverty in Reading concluded that it was not ill-health, broken families or improvidence that was causing distress among the poorest, but simply inadequate wages.[39]

The workhouse

St Mary's parish workhouse on Coley Street had been part of the Coley landscape long before the courts and passages were built in the 1810s and 1820s. In 1758 the parish of St Mary decided that they needed a workhouse of their own, despite the existence of the Oracle only half a mile away. The Oracle had never really functioned efficiently as a workhouse and the Vestry agreed to look for a suitable location. By 1760 they had settled upon premises in Pigney's Lane belonging to a John Ward. Three hundred pounds was spent to modify the building and make it 'convenient for the use of the poor to dwell in'. Not long afterwards it was decided that this adapted building was not appropriate; it was demolished and a whole new workhouse built, which opened in 1772.[40] Frederick Eden, writing in 1797, said the building had cost £1400, of which only £650 had been paid off by then.[41]

The building was divided into separate lodging rooms and could house about 90 people. It was here that the poor would gather for relief, either a payment in hand or (much more commonly) admittance into the workhouse. These scenes must have been tense, one old Reading resident reminisced:

> at the time it was the custom for able-bodied men to apply at the workhouses and demand money, and by threats of violence they often obtained some.[42]

Eden comments that generally the house was occupied by the very young and the very old. There, those that could would be put to work, spinning hemp, weaving sailcloth or labouring with the farmers. The workhouse seems to have been basic but adequate, and he lists the diet:

Day of the week	Breakfast	Dinner	Supper
Sunday	Bread, cheese and beer	Meat, pudding, vegetables and bread	Bread, cheese and beer
Monday	Bread and broth	Bread and cheese	Ditto
Tuesday	Milk pottage	Bread and broth	Ditto
Wednesday	Milk pottage	Cold meat	Ditto
Thursday	Bread and cheese	Same as Sunday	Ditto
Friday	Bread and broth	Cold meat	Ditto
Saturday	Milk Pottage	Bread and cheese	Ditto

Old people are allowed tea, bread and butter for breakfast

Extract from Frederick Eden's *State of the Poor*

The 1783 Ratepayer's Census shows a Mrs Thickbroom running the workhouse. St Mary's baptisms show regular entries of legitimate, or, more often, illegitimate babies born to the inmates.

These children were usually farmed out at a very young age to become servants. Sarah Bartholomew told the St Giles overseers in 1843 that she had been picked out at the age of 10 by Mr Cumber, the master of St Mary's, to work as servant in Stratfield Mortimer.

John Berkeley Monck took an active interest in the Poor Law, and seems to have taken quite a hands-on role in terms of their management in the workhouse. Those that were directly helped by money from him were obliged to wear the letters 'MP' on their uniform, standing for 'Monck's Poor'.

The 1834 Poor Law Amendment Act meant the amalgamation of the three parishes into one Reading Union. A board of 15 guardians was established, five from each parish, and at one of its earliest meetings in August 1835 they decided to close the St Giles workhouse, keep open St Mary's as a general poorhouse, looking after the young, sick and elderly, and St Laurence's as a workhouse for the able-bodied poor.

Grey uniforms were to be worn, and boots and shoes supplied. The regime was strict, and disorder or non-cooperation often led to an appearance before the magistrate. Drinking was frowned upon, and the view among the temperance-influenced worthies of the town was that drink was the primary reason that most found themselves there. In January 1842 an inquest investigated the death of a John Edgerton who refused to enter St Mary's workhouse, despite being on the verge of starvation, as he believed he would not be let out. Mr Frederick West, the master of St Mary's, testified that paupers were normally let out on a Saturday, but Mr Edgerton had come back so often intoxicated he had been prevented from doing so. The workhouse seems to have been used as a hospital for the poor, where vagrants found injured or dying were brought, instead of to the Royal Berkshire Hospital.

When the census was taken in 1841 there were 106 people in the workhouse, 68 women and 38 men; 18 of the men were over the age of 60, while 23 of the women were under the age of 30.

By the 1860s the workhouse was inadequate for the growing population of Reading, and it was reported that men were sleeping two abed. By 1865 the Reading Union had bought the site along the Oxford Road, and in September 1868 the old and frail of St Mary's were the last to be moved into the new workhouse.

The old workhouse was immediately modified to become the new home for the Ragged School, but this was not to last long as Forster's 1870 Education Act soon provided for a new Board School at the other end of Coley Street.

The building was then adapted to become the Coley Hall and after 1875 a British Workman's Institute was added next door.

Attached to the building, Union Square was built, named after the old Union workhouse.

In the 20th century the building was again reinvented as a boys' club, which it continued to be well into the 1950s and 1960s, long after Union Square disappeared. One former club member remembers it as a 'sinister building', with the windows high up in the walls. It was eventually demolished in the 1960s along with the rest of Coley Street, almost 200 years after it was built.

The School

The Castle and Coley Hill area of Reading had a number of schools over the course of the 18th and into the 19th century. Many of them were small private establishments, such as Miss Welch's School for Young Ladies on Coley Hill, which housed 5 teachers, 28 girls aged 10–18 and 2 servants in 1841, according to the Census.

However, the hundreds of children of Old Coley would not have had any formal schooling at this time, unless they were taken into the workhouse where they would have been taught bible classes and basic literacy. The Rev. Sherman's wife ran a Sunday School in the 1830s where 'every child capable of leaving home was sent'. But this does not seem to have outlasted her tenure.

The first attempt to establish any sort of more general schooling was instigated by 'young men connected with the Castle St. Chapel' in October 1859. It was part of the Ragged School movement founded 15 years previously in London.

It attempted to provide free education for children who were often characterised as 'street urchins' or 'gutter children'. Attendance was patchy and part-time. The first Ragged School in Coley took the form of a Sunday School in an 'ex-beer house in Coley Terrace', which quickly became too small for the purpose.[43]

In December 1860 Alderman Exall, who co-owned the Reading Iron Works located just over the Holybrook, offered two rooms 'on his premises'; it is not clear where these were except that Exall fitted them up and 'made openings by means of stairs onto Coley St'.

By 1862 there were 120 boys on its books, and girls 'slightly exceeded' this number. However, only an average of about 30 boys (and, one assumes, about the same number of girls) attended at any one time. There was a roster of five male teachers and seven female teachers, who gave their time without pay.

By this time it was an evening school. The children who attended were described as 'lawless', their conduct 'almost unendurable'. Sympathy was expressed for these children, however, who would 'work from a very early hour and when night comes they find themselves jaded and without heart for vigorous effort.'[44]

It was clear that only a day school would properly cater for the children's needs.

By 1870 Exall's premises were no longer available. Fortunately, the old workhouse had just been closed and the old building lay empty. The premises were bought for £300 and converted for a further £324, transforming the pauper dormitories into two schoolrooms, 120 boys in one and 120 girls in the other, divided by a partition.

At its opening the school is described as 'very nicely decorated, and the walls hung with numerous pictures and maps'.[45]

This was the opportunity to move to become a day school, which meant the building could also be used as a Sunday School, Evening Reading Room and Band of Hope Temperance meeting place, as well as a soup kitchen when needed in this 'hitherto neglected and almost destitute neighbourhood'.[46]

The symbolism of the conversion was not lost on the many speakers at the opening, one Mr Colebrook noting that through education there should be 'less need of gaols and workhouses'.[47]

Eight days after the Mayor opened the building, a bill was introduced into Parliament for the provision of secular, elementary education for all children. Forster's Education Act was passed in the August of that year. Reading set up its own School Board in 1871, John Bligh Monck being a founding member.

The aim of the Act was to provide education where it was inadequate, and Katesgrove, Coley and Silver Street were early priorities. Schools were taken over and adopted by the Board, but in October of that year it was noted that Coley School was 'not up to the requirement of the Act, (and) the School Board have not yet taken possession'.[48]

In November the school board finally took possession and agreed on a £100 annual salary for the master and mistress.

In December they appointed the first teachers: Mr Bibby, Master for the Boys, Miss Lush, Mistress for the Girls, and Mrs Thatcher (already 64) for the infants.

On 15 January 1872 the first intake started at the Coley Board School. Altogether 92 children, boys, girls and infants down to age 3, arrived on the first day.[49]

These 92 children were only a small proportion of the children who should have been attending. The fees of 2d for the first child, and a penny for any subsequent, were simply too much for some families, and charitable provision had to be made for some families before their children could attend. In addition, many of the older girls were kept at home to look after small babies. Gradually more children enrolled as the attendance officer visited families and provision was made. By the end of the year there were around 250 children attending the school, although numbers fluctuated.

Teachers and monitors were taken on to break down the numbers into smaller groups, but their quality was questionable, and they often had time off for ill health. The noise and disruption caused by around 100 children in one room, not used to learning, and with any number of what were termed 'backward children' at one time, would horrify a modern teacher. The school, like all the new board schools, was subject to frequent visits and inspection, usually several times a week. Mr. Bibby complained that 'The children continue to take advantage when visitors are in the room, being at such times the most noisy.'

An inspection in December 1872 found tremendous overcrowding, with '97 or 98 boys round the master, when the number should be limited to 90. On some occasions ... there had been as many as 106'. Meanwhile 'the accommodation for the increasing number of infants is absolutely insufficient'. The old workhouse, despite the positive write-up in the local paper, was clearly unsuitable as a school. There was no real playground, the only outside space 'being covered in large stones'.[50]

The damning December 1872 report led in January 1873 to a decision to find suitable sites for new Coley and Katesgrove schools. A three-quarters of an acre site belonging to the 'trustees of the late Mr James Bushnell' who had owned Little Coley Farm was identified at the end of Coley Street.

The site cost £750 and a further £5,540 9s 6d was to be spent on the building. The contract went to the Wheeler Brothers who owned Coley Kiln. The school was finished by the summer of 1874

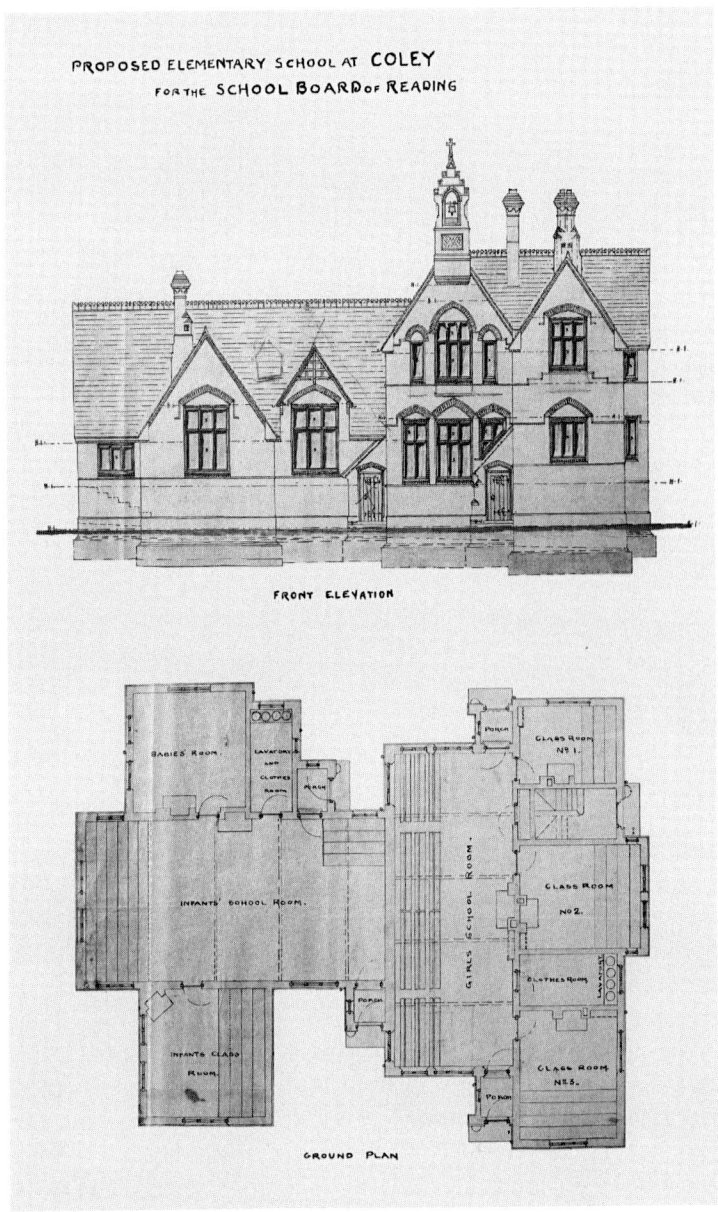

Plans for Coley School, 1873

Coley School today

and the children and teachers 'resumed duties in the new school' on 3 August that year.

The Inspector's report that December stated that 'the new buildings are thoroughly satisfactory'. More space meant that babies were taken in below the age of 3, which meant older girls were more able to attend school regularly.

The new facilities, a gradual increase in teacher numbers and growing acceptance by the community of the need for education led to a consistent improvement in standards. By the time our interviewees can remember, the 1930s and 1940s, it was a thriving and much-loved school.

Community, religion, pastimes and politics

Commentators looking back at the Coley of the late 19th and early 20th century frequently use the term 'close-knit'. Phoebe Cusden, writing in 1977 of a community of 30 or 40 years before, stated:

> For all its poverty and squalor, the Coley we are concerned with became a closely-knit, self-contained neighbourhood of humble households near the centre of Reading, but isolated *from* the town by the clannish attitude of the local people who regarded everybody outside the area as a foreigner.[51]

This is reflected in the reminiscences of our interviewees, who characterised Coley as being especially deprived and clannish; as Mr W. says, only a few other smaller communities matched Coley.

> Silver Street, Hosier Street and Coley. Other than that, no-one, they would not be in our league at all.

Partly this was a reaction to the reputation Coley had across the town. A fight at a carnival reported in the *Reading Observer* in 1874 started because two ladies 'turned up their noses at Coley people'.[52]

The reputation of Coley was long-standing. Mary Russell Mitford, in her studies of Reading life in the 1830s, describes a warning from an old woman to a young lady about to walk through Coley (which she calls 'Denham') not to get 'into the way of those Denham chaps, especially those Lanes, who are no better than so many poachers and vagrants'.[53]

Of course, where there were working men, there were pubs. Towards the end of the 19th century there were at least 12 in Coley's cramped streets and courts. Just along Coley Street were the Spotted Cow, the Coachmaker's Arms, the Rose and Crown and the Turners Arms. At the beginning of Wolseley Street was the Blue Lion, and further up near the school, the Brickmaker's Arms. Up Coley Passage was the Wooden Walls of Old England; the Hit and Miss in Martha Place; at the top in Coley Place were the John Bull, the Crown and the Bricklayers Arms, and in Willow Street, The Borough Arms. While these were often places for fencing stolen goods and fomenting arguments, they also provided a place to meet and were centres for outings and clubs. The Blue Lion in particular acted as a makeshift coroner's court on many occasions.

The 'urban village' title can be misleading, evoking an insular, unchanging and homogenous population. In fact, Coley, like many poor, urban areas, was a centre of migration, the first port of call for those who came looking for work in Reading. In 1841 nearly 20 per cent of Coley's population was born outside of Berkshire, and a considerable number more (not counted in the census) would have come from outside Reading. Coley had several lodging houses, one being 2a Coley Street, which in 1841 housed 22 migrant labourers, many from Ireland.

A boarding house in Coley Place in 1901 was run by 63-year-old Luigi Carine, born in Italy. The boarders included four 'ice cream hawkers' (it is possible Carine ran an ice-cream business) from Ireland, Devon, Canada and Liverpool. Three other boarders were from Liverpool, Wantage and Burghfield.

Neighbourhood disputes were often resolved on the streets with violence. In 1861 the master of St Mary's workhouse asked for extra policing in the area 'during the evenings of Saturday and Sunday, when quarrels invariably took place'.[54]

Many in the community did not respond well to the intervention of the law – a riot involving about 100 people started when a policeman attempted to arrest a Coley woman in 1897.

However, as with most communities, they had their own standards and were more than willing to co-operate with the police when they felt they were breached. Emma and Charles Hamblin, who arrived in Coley sometime after 1891, are a good example. From the outset they proved drunken and quarrelsome neighbours, as ready to take others to court as to be taken to court themselves. A string of court appearances appeared in the papers, covering cruelty to animals, drunkenness, obstruction, bad language and poaching. In April 1898 Charles was sentenced to 14 days hard labour for fighting. Emma took the opportunity to walk out on him, abandoning the children, and moved in with another man. The neighbours called the police after the children were left crying and wandering the streets, the oldest, Harriet, 13, looking after the others. It was neighbours who testified in court against the family. Somehow Emma and Charles patched things up, but Charles was banned from the Rose and Crown and the Coachmakers Arms for smashing windows when they refused to serve him. In 1902 they had such a fight that Emma was left 'senseless' on Coley Street. A policeman managed to arrest Charles after a struggle, but then had to contend with 50 Coley men who wanted to throw Hamblin in the Kennet.[55]

A sad footnote to this story is that Harriet, at 15, was deemed to be in moral danger, taken away and put into a Magdalen Laundry in Brighton, appearing as a 'penitent' and washerwoman in the 1901 census.

Drink was considered one of the great evils of communities such as Coley, and the British Workman was an attempt to deal with it. As a movement it was linked to the *British Workman Review* newspaper, which promoted temperance and self-help. Mrs Hind Smith, the editor, addressed the inaugural meeting in Coley Hall (the old Workhouse) in 1875.

The British Workman's Institute, built next to the old Workhouse, became a core community centre for Coley, home to political meetings and clubs, including the football club. The 'Drunken Seven' band was remembered accompanying the football club to matches on the Coley Recreation Ground. The British Workman was keen to distance itself from the band however, going to the lengths of taking an ad in the paper to say its home was the Rose and Crown, and not the BWI.[56]

A further impetus to the temperance movement came in 1881, when the Salvation Army were granted the lease of a boathouse on Fobney Street off Willow Street. At some point 'sinister forces' (presumably brewers) put pressure on the Great Western Railway, who were the landlords, to rescind the lease. They were forced out, and held their meetings on a piece of open ground on Willow Street, which they already owned.[57] The roughs of Coley did not take well to the Salvation Army's open-air meetings and they were forced to use Coley Hall as a temporary home. However, they quickly raised the money to build their own 'barracks', which were opened on 6 December 1881 in Willow Street. Ironically, the GWR took possession of this when it became the goods station for the newly opened Coley Branch line in 1909.

After 1865 a new evangelical zeal in the Church of England saw it setting its sights on poorer communities, and in St Mary's that meant Coley. The Rev. Garry arrived at St Mary's in 1875 and quickly established a 'Mission Room' in Coley, which seems to have been

St Saviours Church

on the corner of Willow Street and Coley Street. By 1877 he had negotiated with the School Board for the use of land belonging to the school. Here, at the end of a modern playground, an iron church was opened in 1877. Iron churches were used to a great extent across Reading at this time and were a cheap way of providing places of worship within communities that would otherwise struggle to support them. Coley folk could not afford the donations, subscriptions and pew rents that paid for newly built churches elsewhere. The iron church, St Saviour's, served the community for ten years, but when Coley Kiln moved from land at the end of Wolseley Street, a rather grander, brick-built building was started. The new St Saviour's opened in 1887, largely paid for by the wider St Mary's parish. The iron church was packed on to a wagon to become St Mark's on the Oxford Road.[58]

Nonetheless all denominations struggled to keep attendance up in the streets of Coley, at least among the working men. In 1904 a meeting was held at St Saviour's entitled 'Why men do not attend church or chapel'. Councillor Jones addressed the meeting, saying:

> The absence of men from places of worship is due in the main to social conditions which render attendance almost impossible.[59]

Men did not want to spend their scant leisure time being lectured to about temperance and hard work. Children attended, however, and Sunday School treats were to be big feature of Coley life well into living memory.

Politics and representation

In 1826, with a population of approximately 800, there were 26 voters in Coley.[60]

This is a high number in comparison with other areas in the UK at the time. In Reading, pre-1832, simply paying your poor rate qualified you to vote. Thus we see bakers, carpenters and shoemakers from Pigney's Lane and Coley Terrace turning out to vote in 1826.

After the Great Reform Act of 1832 and the introduction of the property qualification, the electorate of Coley actually diminished slightly, so despite the growth in population there were only 25 voters in 1837. As there was no secret ballot at this time, we know these 25 voted overwhelmingly for the Whigs. This is not surprising given their demand for electoral reform, and the political persuasion of the local gentry, the Moncks.

The great extension of the franchise, the 'leap in the dark' as Lord Derby described it at the time, was the 1867 Reform Act that allowed all urban male householders, renters or owners, to vote, as long as they had been in situ for 12 months. Lodgers could also vote if they paid more than £10 a year. This immediately nearly quadrupled the voters in Coley, from 29 in January 1868 to 106 in November when the new register was completed.

Those in receipt of poor relief or paying less than £10 lodging fee were still ineligible, which seems to have excluded more than half the adult males. Inflation, and possibly some improvement in the properties, meant rents rose over time, gradually tipping more into the franchise. By 1878 there were 256 voters in Coley; partly explained by expansion, but also those newly enfranchised in the old courts and passages.

Across Reading the electorate went from 1,503 in 1859 to 4,721 in 1878. That, and the introduction of the secret ballot in 1872, meant that political campaigning had to move onto a whole new footing. Out were the feasts and treats for voters, expecting to see a return at the ballot, and in came public meetings with candidates and their supporters out on the stump in church and school halls across the town. In 1885 Reading became a single member constituency and successive elections were won and lost on little more than a hundred votes. Places like Coley were to become hard-fought battlegrounds.

In 1918 the pauper disqualification was removed and all men over 21 and women over 30 got the vote. By 1919 Coley housed about 1,800 voters.[61]

Representation was not confined to parliamentary elections. Not only were there elections to the Town Council, but also Poor Law Guardians, and, after 1870, the School Board. In local government the franchise was a lot larger – all male ratepayers from 1835 and single women ratepayers from 1868. Then, as now, Coley was part of the Minster Ward, at this time actually covering the old Minster area, including the Butts and Gun Street. Minster Ward is the oldest ward in the town, one of the original medieval wards, appearing as early as 1440 as 'Mynstreward'.[62]

The Town Council in the late 19th century was dominated by upper- and middle-class interests, local businessmen and the mighty Ratepayers Association, which worked to keep spending, and thus rates, as low as possible. This severely hindered work to improve conditions in Coley. Representatives for Minster Ward were often prominent businessmen such as Daniel Heelas. Political affiliation is difficult to establish, as this was still somewhat frowned on in local policymaking, and the pretence of neutrality was maintained, even when electoral organisation was obviously handled by either Liberals or Conservatives.

In the 1880s a Reading branch of the Marxist Social Democratic Foundation (SDF) was established, and the first avowed 'socialist', Harry Quelch, returned in Katesgrove.[63]

Minster elected their own socialist representative in Sam Jones, a bricklayer from Coley Street in 1900. From the outset Councillor Jones focused on improving the living conditions of the poor of the town, including Coley. He was hampered in his work by the fact that most council meetings were held during the day, and he had to earn a living. A fraught exchange at a meeting in 1902 had him berate the Council about their lack of action on improving living conditions. He was accused of grandstanding by a Councillor Bonney, who said the proper place to raise these issues was at the Sanitary Committee, which he rarely attended. 'Adopt evening meetings and I will attend as many as you!' he replied. In 1901 he was joined by Patrick Connolly, a Coley biscuit factory employee, who was supported by the Worker's Electoral League. He encountered similar problems with daytime meetings. In 1902 they were joined by Thomas Waters, a keen trade unionist who lived in St Mary's Butts.

Three 'socialist' councillors in three years indicates an impressive level of organisation and campaigning. The SDF ran a continuing campaign against Huntley and Palmers and their labour relations policies. The biscuit factory, or the ancillary Huntley, Bourne and Stevens, by this time employed about one quarter to a third of the working people of Coley, who seem, by the votes the councillors gained, to have supported the action.

Jones was re-elected in 1903, despite considerable organisation against him. Connolly was re-elected in 1904. In 1905 John Rabson replaced Waters.

Minster was the only ward on the council to return three socialist members simultaneously. In November 1905 the Council agreed to allow its monthly meetings to be held in the evening. However it continued to be dominated by those more interested in saving money than spending it.

The councillors were supported in much of their work by Lorenzo Quelch, brother to Harry, who worked with them to organise the unemployed in 1908. Quelch was elected to the Council for Minster in 1914. He was not a Coley man, having been born in Hungerford, and lived most of his years in Reading in Gower Street.

The *Reading Mercury* referred to him as 'Battling Quelch', and he was relentless in his fights to obtain work and relief for the unemployed in Coley. In 1916 he helped to organise the strike of the

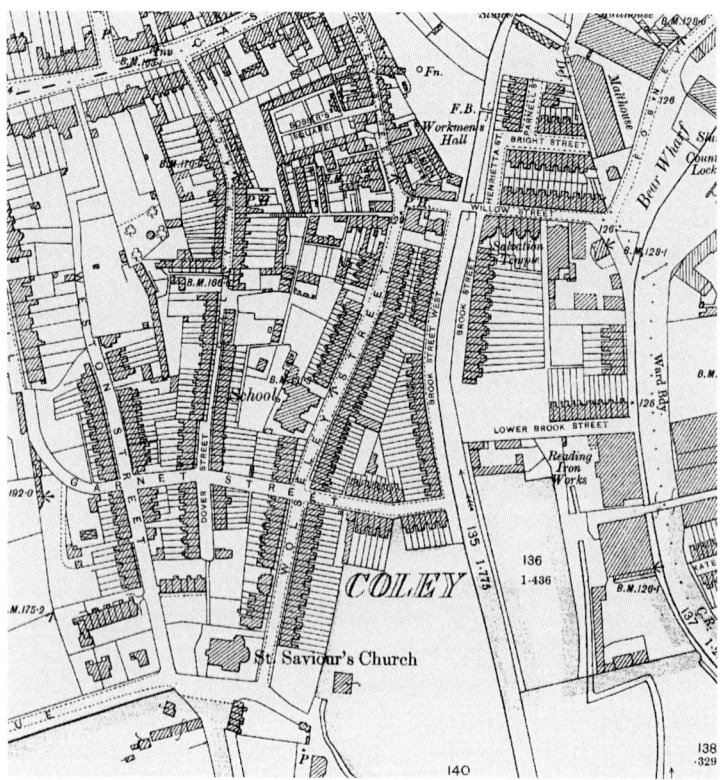

Coley in 1900

female staff at Huntley and Palmers. The *Mercury* described him as having the appearance of a

> comfortable easy going retired gentleman by his large-brimmed soft hat, conspicuous tie and leisurely demeanour as he moves along Friar St. on his way to Oxford Road (HQ of the Labour Council) solacing him at all times by a well-seasoned briar.[64]

His speech style was described as 'concise, plain-speaking and very hard hitting at times. He knows the power of sarcasm'. He was used to open air meetings and could command a gathering from the back of a wagon. In 1917 he became a JP.

Reading Labour Party did not officially form until 1918, and after that time election campaigns quickly became straight battles between Labour and Conservatives, with the Liberals swiftly disappearing from contention. Dr Somerville Hastings, Reading's first Labour MP, was returned in 1922. Our interviewees remembered the tribalism, chanting and open conflict associated with election campaigns of the day, scenes we would more normally associate with a local derby football match.

Changes in Coley, 1890–1910

In 1884 John Bligh Monck offered land on his estate to the Corporation for £300 an acre (it was valued at £500 an acre as building land) or £10 a year rental with an option to buy. The land was to be used as a recreational area for Coley. Opinion was divided as some councillors thought it inappropriate and too expensive. Nonetheless the recreation ground was agreed, improved with the planting of trees and layout of pitches, and opened to the public in 1890. In 1903 Bligh Monck died at the age of 91, and his son, William Berkeley, already 60, inherited. His tenure was short-lived, as less than two years later in 1905 he was accidentally shot and killed on his estate by his son, George Stanley.

In 1908 the GWR compulsory-purchased a swathe of land through Coley and to Southcote for the Coley branch line. It opened as a spur from the Basingstoke line to Southcote, intended for goods serving breweries and brick kilns in the area. This involved the purchase

Coley Goods Station, which had been the Salvation Army temple.

and repurposing of the Salvation Army Temple in Willow Street, and George Stanley Monck received about £7,000 compensation for the impact on his land (considerably less than the £17,000 he had originally claimed). George then sold off portions of land around Berkeley Avenue to Reading Corporation. Finally, Berkeley Avenue linked up to Katesgrove by a road crossing the Holybrook and joining Elgar Road. In 1915 a small aerodrome was opened there for training the Royal Flying Corps. The branch line made it suitable for light industry, with the cws Jam Works opening in 1919 and Gascoigne Milking Machines opening in 1927. Coley Swimming Baths were built in the loop of the Holybrook, off what today is Laud Close, in 1910.[65]

II. Talking of living conditions

'Those who know the "Steps" find it difficult to condone the actions of those who planned the houses and courts with such unconcern for the well-being of the hundreds who were herded together in conditions regardless of comfort and decency.'
—Rev. G.R. Webster
   The History of St Saviour's Church and District, 1939

The houses in Coley at the opening of the 20th century represented a range from the semi-rural cottages on the south side of Berkeley Avenue and the late Victorian model artisan terraces of Wolseley Street and Field Road (then Weston Road) to the cramped and insanitary courts and back-to-backs around Coley Passage.

Mr A. moved to Coley Kiln Cottages in 1918. These cottages were opposite the recreation ground in St Saviour's Road, then still largely open fields. His father was a painter and decorator and therefore classed as a skilled labourer; his mother took in washing. He writes:

> Our home was the end of a row of cottages. The accommodation comprised a small scullery, a living room and three bedrooms. Our front room was special and only really used at Christmas. We had an outside toilet which had a proper flush! I remember our living room always being warm. It was heated by a kitchen range in the winter and we cooked on it during this time. In summer we used the gas cooker for cooking. In winter the bedrooms were freezing... We were expected to help our father in our large garden where we grew all our own vegetables and flowers... We ate vegetables fresh from the garden. We also bred rabbits for food.

Built later, but similar in many respects excepting the large garden, were the houses at the St Saviour's end of Wolseley Street, the 'posh end of Coley'. Mrs N. moved to 155 Wolseley Street in 1909 and remembered:

> Well the house that – I expect you've seen them, they're two bay windowed houses, and they're white houses... they're still painted white. You went in the front room and the stairs went

straight up the side, it was really a nice house. There was a front room and then you went into the kitchen and then you went through the kitchen and into the scullery ... and then you walked out the back door and there was a nice porch and there was the toilet on one side all under cover and the coal-house the other.

The more common pattern, and one repeated in most housing of its type throughout Reading, exists further down Wolseley Street. Some houses have tiny front gardens; some open directly onto the street. The slightly bigger houses have a small entrance hall, whilst others open into the front room. A staircase goes up between the front room and the back room. In those days the back room was the main living area, with a range where most of the cooking was done. Then came the scullery with a stone sink and a large copper-lined tub in the corner, usually referred to as the 'copper'. This had an area underneath for a fire. Water was then boiled up in this either for washing clothes or for bath water. The room may also have had a gas cooker – although for economic reasons this was normally only used in the summer – and a mangle for drying out clothes. None of these houses had bathrooms when they were built.

Although many people at the time aspired to keeping the front room special, few of these households could do so. Often it was converted to another use, such as one of the many 'front-room' type shops that existed in Coley.

Mr A. (born 1916) Well the front room was like a little shop.

Int. What did it sell?

Mr A. Well more or less all the little things of everyday needs ... like sweets and a little grocery, stuff like that.

Alternatively, the front room may have been converted to another bedroom. There was a fireplace in the front room, but this was rarely lit. Downstairs the lighting was either gas or paraffin lamps; the upstairs was lit by candles and there was no heating. Some houses had two bedrooms, some three, with the third bedroom leading off the second. Families of six, seven or eight children were quite common in Coley up to and including the inter-war period, so it was often necessary for three or more children to share a bed – although great lengths were taken to separate boys and girls. The youngest, or more rarely, the two youngest children, might sleep with the parents and it was not unheard of for older children to be put out to relatives in the area.

However, the people who lived in these houses were only too aware that they lived in relative comfort compared to the people who lived off Coley Passage, or in the areas such as Bosier Square or Commercial Hall.

Mrs C. and Mrs N. are sisters born in 1908 and 1910 respectively. They lived with their father and mother, two brothers and two other sisters in 4 Hazel Court off Coley Passage. Their father had chronic bronchitis and was unable to work for long periods. Their mother took in washing and did some cleaning to support the family. The houses were the back-to-back type and had no through ventilation. They had no water, no toilets and no copper. These were outside and were all shared with other houses.

> *Mrs C.* There were four houses with one toilet, down there, and that's where the copper was, what we all had to share, to burn rubbish up for our mums to do the washing.

The toilets had no flush, so a bucket of water had to be collected from the standpipe for the purpose. The ground floor of the houses consisted of one room only.

> *Int.* Was there a kitchen?

> *Mrs N.* No we didn't have a kitchen, no.

> *Mrs C.* We just had what they called a coal cellar then for a fire, and that was in the little room that we all had to live. Paraffin lamps on the table at nights, you know.

> *Int.* So what did your mum do her cooking on then?

> *Mrs C.* Mum used to do her cooking on the fireplace [on a range]... on the top we had one pot boil up and [you] just pull[ed] it along so – because we had an oven in there as well.

The oven, however, was quite small, and like a lot of Coley people this family took any bulky baking or cooking, such as a rare cut of meat, to Darvall's the Bakers to be cooked for a penny.

The Coley Steps c1910

The living room was seven feet high and had lino on the floor with some straight-backed chairs, a table, and a sofa which was made into a bed for the eldest boy. Upstairs was a bedroom used by the mother and father and the younger boy, and above that an attic that the four girls used as a bedroom.

> *Mrs C.* We had two beds in our room. Mum had us four girls then. Our Flo, Bessie and Nan and our Alice used to have a little single one, the eldest one on her own and we just squeezed in like... we used to call it up the garret.
>
> *Int.* It must have got quite hot up there?
>
> *Mrs N.* It was, yes, because it had a slanting roof... you know... one window – you couldn't feel the air much.

When it was very hot the girls slept in the front garden.

> *Mrs C.* We used to lay out there on a double blanket with a bit of mat underneath it and wind the cover over us, and we used to sleep out there in the garden night times.

Mr F. lived at 1 Poplar Court and was born in 1921.

> *Mr F.* I remember when my mother lit the paraffin lamp at dusk, the cockroaches swarmed across the floor in droves. They seemed immune to Keaton's Powder. We had our heads cut bald because of fleas.

There were also rats:

> We had a good dog, but he could not catch all the rats.

Like Hazel Court there were two bedrooms, one on top of the other.

> *Mr F.* Yes, me mum and dad slept in one, and I shall always remember us all having mumps and we was all in bed together... at that time there would have been five boys.

Getting water from the tap was not always straightforward.

> *Mr F.* In winter times it was very hard. There was only one standpipe and people had to light a lot of paper until it thawed out. Very often there was a large queue; I don't know how many people went without a morning drink.

People from the rest of Coley used to help out.

> *Mrs N.* We had those terrible winters ... then of course they had to rely on people to go and take them buckets of water.

However, Mr F. considered himself 'fortunate' because the pipe was only just outside his house, unlike some who had to climb up and down steps with their water.

Mr B. was born in 1919 and lived in Commercial Hall. The houses here did have a copper in the basement but were similar in other respects.

> *Mr B.* There was no taps or water provided to the house. In fact, there was only one water stand between six houses up where we were, and that was an outside tap which froze up at the first sign of winter ... the other tap was down below the bottom of Commercial Hall, which was another 21 steps down, and that was an outside tap as well. And by that time we worked it in sequence; all the families around de-freezing the taps until we got water to provide all the remainder. And there was plenty! You used the outdoor stand for all facilities: cooking, washing and all cleaning of the house. All toilets were the outdoor type way up at the end of the garden. We had three toilets between six and it was a job when one happened to walk in with a newspaper – you were there for life!

Mr D. was born in 1909 and spent his early years in Bosier Square. He writes about his impression of the place:

> Laundry washing consisted of a cast iron boiler under a rusty tin roof, one water tap, in some instances cesspits that overflowed. We did our best to keep clean and despite the weather were made to strip out ... in many cases these hovels had rats for company, the cats were well fed due to the swarms of mice. As if this was not enough the other vermin would be in attendance – bed bugs and fleas of course ... and head lice. [Another problem] during the summer [were the] hundreds of flies and, as a bonus, cockroaches.

Already poorly constructed, the buildings were allowed to fall into disrepair. People told stories of landlords repairing holes with old boxes, and whole walls collapsing in the middle of the night. Mr F. remembered:

> Well it was like sort of made with a few bricks ... you might have had, say, about four bricks high, and then you had wood, you know, timber in between that, then built up again a bit further and then timber again. And the mortar, well, the mortar was just like dry sand, I mean after all them years, because they were condemned ... and you could see why afterwards, because you could put your finger on the wall and you could push it out.

The people who lived there seemed to demonstrate a resigned acceptance to the conditions, but are amazed in retrospect at what they put up with.

> *Mr F.* It's incredible when you think that you lived in a place where you never had no light, you know, where you had to light a paraffin lamp and you never had no water.

The slums made a deep impression on outsiders who saw them.

> *Mr T.* There was houses there, I always remember going along there, and there were just the small rooms and a table.

> *Mr K.* Oh, it was terrible.

> *Mr T.* And a table and a candle, frightening really... nothing in there.

> *Mr K.* Dreadful place.

Mr E. was a junior architectural assistant involved in surveying Bosier Square in 1933, shortly after the residents had been moved out to Whitley. He recalls most vividly the impression these houses made on him at the time, merely weeks before they were, at last, demolished:

> I was about twenty years old and this was my first experience of slum housing conditions and I have never forgotten my first sense of shock at the discovery of the conditions under which some people lived. Since the houses were of the back-to-back variety, as was common in northern mill towns in Victorian

days, there was no possibility of through ventilation and the smell was revolting – although this was probably aggravated by the buildings having been unoccupied for some weeks. The 'decoration' consisted of patches of damp and dirt highlighted by bloodstains where bugs had been squashed. The condition of the communal lavatories was indescribable, and I well remember I was unable to face meals whilst engaged on this work.

Keeping a family fed and clean, and a house sanitary and comfortable, must have been a mammoth task under these circumstances. However, the surprising cleanliness of the children from the slums was remarked on. For example, an inspector's report in one of the Coley School log books states:

The children ... attend in a clean and tidy condition

A local person comments:

Some of the children were absolutely spotless.

Mr D. of Bosier Square wrote:

One only had to see the girls in their white pinafores and neatly darned stockings, us boys with neatly patched trousers, even

Coley, c1930, during the demolition of the slums, looking down from Coley Place to the Blue Lion on Wolseley Street.

if, as was often the case [they were] someone else's, cut-down; our boots polished with Day and Martin's boot-black – these too were often patched. These people were not dirty, no, the odds were stacked against them.

It is difficult to see how the occupants of the Steps could possibly have managed a bath, with no means of heating the water apart from an outside communal copper. Instead, strip washing was the normal procedure, augmented by regular dips in the Holybrook. In the other housing in Coley, baths were a regular feature of Friday night.

> *Mr T.* Bath night we had a long, galvanised bath. It used to stand on the bricks outside there and that was on Friday night and I know our three boys, I mean the eldest one used to get in there first, then the second one, that's Leslie, and Gordon always used to moan because he was last in. It wasn't so clean because you couldn't have three lots of water. It took a long time to get your bath filled up and then that was all over ... and then I used to up-end the bath, put it to the back-brick – that used to wash the back-bricks down with water.

Housework could be both physically strenuous and immensely time-consuming. Of course, there were no vacuum cleaners, washing machines or electric irons. Clothing was more difficult to clean and iron, and cleaning materials were basic: carbolic soap or washing soda and occasionally such things as vinegar and bicarbonate of soda. Items such as grates and ranges were made of iron and had to be blackleaded: 'and the blacking! A morning's work!' to prevent rusting and make them shine. Of course, the vast bulk of this work fell upon the mother and, as the family grew, the elder girls.

It was very important that the household should be seen to be clean and a lot of energy was expended on the front of the house.

> *Mrs N.* We had a picture on our wall ... 'if each before his own door swept, the village would be clean'. And every morning – it was either me or my sister ... we had to go out and sweep the front door step, three steps, and then sweep right along the house, you know, along the gutter ... pick it up in a dustpan and brush and put it in the dustbin.

The step was then whitened:

> *Mrs S.* And the front doorstep was always whitened with a powder, you know, and dried to make it nice and white.

Where the floors were lino, they were polished until they shone. Bare boards, as in the worst housing, were scrubbed with carbolic soap, but 'it was an endless job to keep them clean'. Where there were rats, mice and cockroaches little could be done to get rid of them permanently. Poisons might be put down or houses fumigated, but in the courts and alleyways houses were so close together they would simply re-infest each other.

One of the biggest jobs was the weekly wash. People had far fewer clothes than nowadays and would normally be expected to wear the same set of clothes all week, although girls might have a clean pinafore to wear over their clothes. Even so, washing took all day. Where the copper was shared between houses a rota was worked out. Where women had their own copper, washday was always Monday, although:

> *Mr K.* It used to run into Tuesday with six children at home.

> *Mr T.* Friday was out wasn't it, they didn't believe in Friday.

> *Mr K.* No never washed on Friday.

> *Mr T.* That was taboo.

Generally, the routine was this. Dirty clothes might be piled up in the corner of the scullery until washday. On Monday morning the first job was to get the copper lit to heat the water. The children would have been scouting round on the days before to get old wooden boxes from the market or local shops to act as fuel, although household rubbish was also used. The copper was laboriously filled with a bucket from the cold tap and the fire lit, usually before the children went to school. White and coloured garments would be sorted and put to soak and then given a good scrub on the washboard with carbolic soap. Then the whites would be boiled up in the copper and agitated with a copper stick. These would then be taken out and rinsed with a 'blue bag' in the water to bring out the white. With the water perhaps cooling, the coloureds would then be put in the copper, taken out, and rinsed without a blue bag. The washing was put through a mangle and hung out on the line. Although it was not unknown for elder daughters to be kept back from school on washday, children were often apportioned the tasks of stoking the boiler before they went to school or helping with the mangling when they came back.

> *Mr B.* I well remember ... my duty was to stoke up the boiler, and outside we had a great old wooden mangle. We used to take it in turns in turning the big handle around and squeezing all the water out of the sheets. It was always a delight when the sheets were ... hanging on the line and when they were brought back in, because they used to be rinsed in Reckitt's Blue ... when they came in they were still sparkling white.

Of course, once women had finished with their own washing, they very often had to start on somebody else's. Mrs N.'s mother used to take in washing from the Heelas Bedding Department:

> Well in those days it wasn't like the bedding of today. People would send in their feather beds, you see, to be redone. So they used to empty all the feathers out, and the ticks mother used to have to wash ... I can see her now: she used to scrub – Sunlight soap and a scrubbing brush. Some of those ticks, they'd been soiled – all sorts of things. You see in the kitchen we had a brick floor and she had an old mangle and, of course, if you put a pillow case in you know what happens, the air gets into it doesn't it? ... In fact us girls used to help her. She had a great big bath underneath, you know, with rinsing water because it was all ... armwork and, as she put it through the ringer, so the water used to spurt out and it used to run ... all down the bricks.

Where there was back-to-back housing washing would be hung out the front. Ironing was done in the evenings. A pair of heavy flat irons were used; these would be heated on the range, one in use, one being warmed. Spitting was the time-honoured way of telling if the iron was hot enough. Some of the women living on the Steps would sit out in the evenings talking to their neighbours whilst sitting on their sheets and pillowcases to press them.

Food preparation was all from basics: there were no frozen foods and tinned food was too expensive. Many people had allotments that provided the bulk of their vegetables for most of the year – cabbages, beans, turnips, peas, potatoes, carrots and celery being some of the most popular. Quite a few people kept livestock – rabbits and chickens and, out in the cottages, pigs as well. Chickens were kept for eggs and rabbits eaten or sold to Mr Ming the rabbit seller (who would give you back the skin if you wanted it).

> *Mr W.* You never seen a bloke skin a rabbit so quick in all your life!... He used to skin that rabbit, well you would have to go into seconds, it wouldn't be minutes.

At a time when it was estimated that one-tenth of the population of the UK and one-third of the children in poorer districts were malnourished, the people of Coley seem largely to have managed a reasonable diet. The proximity to the countryside, allotments and livestock made them better off than those in slums in the big cities.

Standards varied, however, and there is no doubt that malnourishment existed in the poorer areas, especially towards the beginning of the century. The poorest people seem to have lived on bread and dripping, supplemented, for the children, by free meals from the Southampton Street Feeding Centre. Even the better off had what to us seems a stodgy diet, with suet puddings, bread, dumplings and potatoes to fill the family up. Many of the women would have been in service before they married, or else had helped out a great deal at home, and were experts in managing on very little. Mr B. came from a family of 11 children and his father was often unemployed, but his mother had been a cook before she married. He remembers:

> Middle of the day there was always something provided. A meal that went right round, usually, probably the old pigs' tails, backbones... They were made up into the pea soup... as thick as you could stand a spoon up in... but the speciality we always used to have was, we used to get stale bread, cheapest off wherever we could, and my old Mum was a wizard when she used to bake bread pudding. She'd make these great big tins of bread pudding, one and a half to two inches thick... and [my father] used to get us lots of little murphies, the smallest potatoes – too small to sell – and he used to boil them until they were nice and soft. You could rub the skin off them. So our usual take away was a wedge of bread pudding in one

pocket and a paper funnel full of ... boiled murphies, and a little twist of salt in a little bit of paper on top. We were made for the day.

Breakfast might be a bit of bread and jam, or porridge or some toast:

> Mrs S. If my Mum wasn't very well off she used to give us slices of bread dipped in cold tea. So what was left in the teapot she'd pour that into the saucer and dripped the slices of bread into there, and sprinkled it with sugar and gave us that to eat: that was our breakfast.

Tea, similarly, could be bread and dripping or bread and lard with sugar sprinkled on the top, but lunch was nearly always some sort of stew followed by a filling pudding. Only the older residents of the Steps really remembered going hungry, but most mothers seem somehow to have filled their children up.

Some women also prepared food for the general stores that occupied the front room – curing hams, making toffee apples and brandy snaps or, as in the case of Mrs R.'s mother, faggots and peas:

> In the bitter cold winter we only had one cold tap, and she used to get the pigs' insides and wash them, run them under the tap – cold water. And the big tin bath with the peas... and she was that bitter she'd be blue.

Of course, local hedgerow fruits were abundant in the late summer, and where these were not sold off to the local jam factory they were made into wine 'strong and potent' in the copper or were turned into jam: 'jars and jars of beautiful jam'.

Many mothers also made clothes for the children and the evenings were often spent darning and sewing by the light of the gas mantle; it was the father's job to mend the shoes. Although it wasn't unheard of for men to help around the house, cooking the children's Sunday breakfast, for example, or helping while the mother was laid up with a new baby, the vast bulk of the domestic work fell upon the women. Mr B. comments, 'poor old Mum was never off her knees, scrubbing or baking or taking care'.

> My mother always used to say the men used to go down to the pub and the poor women used to stop at home and do the work.

III. Talking of making ends meet

> 'The wages of unskilled labour are not sufficient in Reading ... to support a family of three or more children.'
> —L. Bowley and A. R. Burnett-Hurst
>   Livelihood and poverty, 1912

In 1899 Seebohm Rowntree made a study of poverty in York in which he outlined what he considered the minimum standard of living. He said a family on this level:

> Must never spend a penny on railway fare or omnibus ... purchase a halfpenny newspaper ... buy a ticket for a popular concert, write letters to absent children, contribute ... to church or chapel ... join sick clubs or trades unions, for children no dolls ... marbles or sweets, for the father no tobacco ... no beer ... should a child fall ill it must be attended by the parish doctor, should it die it must be buried by the parish. Finally, the wage-earner must never be absent from work for a single day.

Maud Pember-Reeves's study of slum conditions in *Round about a pound a week* in 1913 led her to conclude that to achieve this barest minimum a man needed to earn 25s a week to support a family. At the time the average wage for the working man was 30s. In Reading it was 24s 6d. Bowley and Burnett-Hurst suggest a reason for this:

> In Reading, the principal biscuit company ... probably employs directly a quarter or a fifth of the working class. The result is that in Reading there is an unusually large proportion of unskilled workers whose wages are low and probably prevented from rising by the low scales of agricultural wages in Berkshire and Oxfordshire.

About two-thirds of our sample had fathers who were unskilled or semi-skilled labourers; another four families had no income from the father at all, either through unemployment, illness or death (just over a fifth of our sample worked at Huntley and Palmers). Our sample is too small for statistical certainties but it seems reasonable to assume that a large proportion of the population of Coley earned even less than the average for the town, perhaps 20–25s a week.

Although rents and prices in the town may well have been depressed, the Bowley and Burnett-Hurst study still concludes that between 25 and 30 per cent of Reading's working class lived below Seebohm Rowntree's poverty line, compared to a national average of 19 per cent. In Coley it would be reasonable to double this to 50–60 per cent. It was also estimated that 46 per cent of children in Reading lived below the poverty line. Increase this by the same factor and you get a staggering 92 per cent of children in Coley living below the poverty line.

When one considers that the vast majority of the wage-earners were able-bodied men working full-time, one has to agree with the findings of the Bowley and Burnett-Hurst study that the single most common cause of poverty in Reading at the time was simply inadequate wages.

Many were entitled to poor relief. This was administered through the Reading Union, a union of the three parishes of St Giles, St Laurence and St Mary's. In the early years of the 20th century, it would mostly have taken the form of outdoor relief – a money payment rather than entering the workhouse, mainly reserved for the very elderly and infirm. These payments could not possibly have been adequate. An example comes from the Minute Book of the Board of Guardians, 1910–1912. In November 1910 a family consisting of husband, wife and nine children applied for relief as the father was unemployed. The man was granted 12s 6d as the eldest daughter was working and bringing in 6s a week and the mother 1s 6d, this making a bare pound, well below the minimum necessary. However, the Board of Guardians continually laments the high cost of poor relief, through sheer weight of numbers. In Reading as a whole 4,623 families applied for poor relief in the 26 months from March 1911.

The workhouse was the only provision for some. A particularly pathetic tale is of one Charles Preston. In the Coley School log books he appears on 4 May 1900 as follows:

Dear Madam

The attendance committee will be glad if you will admit into your department of Coley Street School a boy named Charles Preston. He is nearly nine years of age, but is very backward and unfit to be admitted to a standard school.

> It is the wish of this committee that he be tried in your school for a month and that they should then receive a short written report respecting him.
>
> He is an adopted child living with Mrs C. of 1 Lime Court and she will bring him to you this morning with the purpose of being admitted.

It appears the school, and possibly his adopted mother, could not cope. On 1 June there is the entry:

> The boy Charles Preston left on 28 May for the workhouse.

He stayed under the care of the Guardians for the next ten years, as an entry in the minute book for 1910 refers to payment being made for a Charles Preston to be shipped to Canada. It seems to have been a popular policy of the time that children under the care of the Board of Guardians should be emigrated to Canada and Australia to go into service or work on farms, and many Reading adolescents were shipped out in this way. In 1921 the workhouse became the Battle Infirmary, having served as a military hospital during the Great War.[66]

Often families would be paid by the Guardians to take in an orphaned child, and it was obviously pot-luck whether they entered a caring family or not. Adoptions were easily arranged, such as the following arrangement by the local vicar. The mother had been taken into what is now Fairmile Hospital; this interviewee's mother agreed to look after the three children with the father paying 5s a week:

> *Mrs N.* Of course he kept up the payment for a month, then he disappeared. The boy went somewhere else and my mother, well, she had all us children and she had Olive and Ivy. I was 15 then I remember, and it was the time in Castle Street when the Poor Law lawyer was there and you could pay him a shilling and go to him and he'd help you. So someone told my mother, 'Go and see this lawyer, they'd know what to do and find the father of these two girls'. And of course, I can remember going with her and he said, 'Well the only way I can help you,' he said, 'the only way we can find the father of these two girls is to put them in the workhouse'. And that was Battle Hospital in

those days. So my mother said 'Certainly not. I was left without a mother when I was ten years old'. She said, 'I certainly won't put two little girls in the workhouse.' So she brought them up as her own.

None of our interviewees remembered receiving outdoor relief, although almost certainly many Coley families did, and it may well be that as young children they were simply not aware, or that being 'on the parish' was such a disgrace that parents didn't talk about it at all.

What people did remember were other forms of Municipal Poor Relief. For example, Board Schools had found that attendances dropped dramatically during bad weather as children did not have adequate footwear. In 1908 free boots were introduced. Mr A. started school about 1910:

Mr A. Never had new clothes, never mind uniform. We used to have to go down just opposite the station ... there used to be a hotel there in Station Road.

Int. The Great Western?

Mr A. Yes, there used to be an Educational Office there ... well when you was a little kid and you used to have nothing, you'd get a ticket from the school and you'd go there and get a pair of boots ... I've been there and come out with a nice pair of hobnailed boots.

There was also the Southampton Street Feeding Centre referred to earlier. It is not clear how people qualified for free meals there, but the rules were obviously stringent since only 512 households in Reading (1,407 children) qualified to send their children there in 1912.

Children were walked down to the Centre at lunchtime by teachers. Mr Ellis, a headteacher at Coley School, complained about this as it made the teachers late for their lessons.

Mr F. Most of my brothers, if they wanted a dinner they had to walk to Southampton Street. There was free dinners, well they used to give you a dinner. You had to get there on time or they didn't give you anything.

The Old British School, Southampton Street, home of the Feeding Centre

Mrs C. started school in 1915:

> You used to go down a long passage to it ... and there was a big place at the back where we all used to go and sit.
>
> *Mrs N.* They used to get a lot of children in there didn't they?
>
> *Mrs C.* I can't remember how many, duck, but I know we wasn't alone going there.

Mr D. writes:

> My dinner was provided on a charity ticket, we being given one each school day by our teacher ... so it was me who went

after morning school to the old British School building in
Southampton Street. These dinners were not bad, consisting
of the usual stew with dumplings followed by stewed prunes,
sometimes jam tart or plum duff. This meal kept us from
completely starving as it was pretty certain that there would
be precious little more until next morning's banquet of stale
bread and buns.

In 1921 1,000 Reading children a day were receiving free meals, either here or at ancillary stations in Tudor Road and Palmer Hall.[67]

Charity was an expected duty of the middle classes in those days and Coley, surrounded as it was by the large houses in Castle Hill and Coley Avenue, got its share. One of the highlights of the year was the Christmas breakfast, paid for by Mr Bucknell of Bucknell's Farm and other local businessmen.

Mr W. In our church (St Saviour's) they used to have a
Christmas breakfast and you used to have to put your
name and address on a piece of paper and the caretaker of
the church, he was a crippled chap who lived round Brook
Street ... he used to put a box up, a letter box, and you put
your name and address on this and that entitled you to a seat
in the church hall at Christmas, for Christmas breakfast. Now
the food came from the people that lived in – Johnny Bucknell
would give a lot, he would bring all the stuff on his carts and
that, down the Sunday School. I remember holding the horse's
head ... hundreds used to turn up to go in. And we used to take
a bag, have the bag under the table, fill the bag while you was
eating, put food so you was purloining.

Children would very often be presented with fruit and sweets on leaving. There seems to have been an unwritten law about which children could apply.

Mrs N. And of course Christmastime the church always gave
a breakfast for two hundred children from the Steps. And
they all used to have their breakfast there at eight o'clock every
Christmas morning. I can remember crying, saying, 'I'd like to
go and have my breakfast there', and my mother said, 'I can
provide you with a breakfast, you're not like those poor little
children, their mothers can't give them a nice breakfast'. And

> I used to watch them coming out and they used to have a bag
> of sweets and a bag of biscuits, and an orange and an apple,
> and perhaps one or two chocolates – something like that.

Mrs N. remembered that Mrs Ward (known in Coley as Lady Ward) also dispensed charity at Christmas:

> Us Bible girls, we used to go up the Steps, and get a plate and
> a basin and a jug, and then we used to go to Lady Ward's into
> the kitchen, and we used to have a Christmas dinner given to
> us on a plate, you know, covered over, and a jug of – I don't
> know how we carried it when I think about it now – and on top
> of the plate was another plate with Christmas pudding you see,
> and a jug of soup, and we used to take that up to the families
> on the Steps …. This was before the 1914 war you see.

On 9 November 1902 the following is entered in the Coley School logbooks: 'Many boys were this morning attending St Laurence's as recipients of clothing, a charity dispensed biennially'. Bowley and Burnett-Hurst sum up the probable effect of these charities on peoples' lives:

> There is a large number of charities and many charitable
> persons in Reading, and it is likely that clothes are often
> obtained. But it is not probable that gifts, doles and subsidies
> lift any large proportion of these people over the line; in
> general they only remove the destitution and leave a deficiency.

As soon as children were able, they would start bringing in money. This was a cause of some concern in 1900 when a directive was sent round to all Board Schools to enquire about outside earnings, which:

> it is believed, is in many cases injurious to their health and
> greatly hindering in their education.

There was plenty of work available for these children. For the boys: working on market stalls, paper rounds, 'spud-picking' in the holidays at Bucknell's Farm; for the girls: looking after babies. Running errands was popular with both. 'We'd run a mile for a halfpenny', one interviewee commented. A particularly common job for the boys in the holidays was 'pricking out' at Simonds Brewery.

Mr T. Pricking out all the week for 5s. I used to do it myself. Pricking out the holes for malt that's laid on the top, yes, 5s a week.... It was a stone floor, perforated with holes and all the malt was spread over there like, and the heat, it was like a steaming process. But they used to have to unblock the holes in these bricks with a cork and a nail on the end – you used to have.

Mr K. Cause you were lying on your stomach.

Mr T. We used to lay on a sack. That was what we were paid, 5s a week.

Children generally left school at 14, although they could take an examination to go on to further education. It was the continual lament of headteachers at Coley School that bright children were not allowed to stay on, as the parents needed their income. It is difficult to blame the parents in the circumstances.

A girl starting work at 14 could earn on average 5s 6d a week in a factory, or 2s plus board and lodgings in service. Although many of the interviewees' mothers had been in service before marriage, none of them themselves had done this. Popular jobs for the girls were doing laundry work or working at Huntley and Palmers.

Boys could earn 6s 6d a week on average at this age. Again, errand work would be popular. Mr A.'s employment history was fairly typical:

As a boy I helped on a market stall selling sweets. I worked 12 hours 8am to 8pm for 2s 6d. I also did a morning and an evening paper round. My first job, when I left school at 14, was at Cross the Chemist in Oxford Road, washing medicine bottles. I was also a labourer in the building trade and helped at the garage at Sutton's Seeds Merchants. I worked with my father who was a painter and decorator until the outbreak of the war.

For many of the older boys the army was an attractive option.

Mothers also used to supplement the family income by taking in washing, doing cleaning jobs, running small businesses from the front room or helping in the local shop. One of the most common forms of supplementing income at the time, taking in lodgers, does not seem to have been all that common in Coley but, as one interviewee remarked wryly, 'The only lodgers we had room for were fleas and cockroaches.'

Families had to be scrupulously economical in everything they did, buying only the cheapest offal, queuing for stale bread and cakes, buying produce late on a Saturday night when prices were knocked down, and scouting round for bargains. One of the perks of working with Huntley and Palmers was the broken biscuits you could take home. These were called 'scranners', which became the local word for Huntley and Palmers.

> *Mr T.* It always amazes me that my wife and E.C. and two of the boys, they walked from here to Wokingham, because in the paper the shoes were cheaper in Wokingham. They walked there to get these shoes for our boys, and back. Walked there, pushed the pram.

Nothing was wasted.

> *Mr W.* We only had a two-wheeled cart – horse and cart – and that cleared the rubbish of Coley. Now can you imagine how big that cart was? It was four foot by five foot ... now there's 16 houses in here – they've got more rubbish out of these 16 houses than you got out of the whole of Coley.

> *Mrs S.* Your mum used to save up all the old rags, grown out clothes and that, and they used to sort them when we got down to Jackson's and they used to put all the woollens on one scale and all the old cottons on the other and they used to give you about a penny or tuppence a pound.

Other rubbish might be burnt on the range or in the copper, and the cinders from there laid down to make paths. Luxuries were few and far between.

> *Int.* Did you get any pocket money?

> *Mr W.* Bought a Mars bar once, spent the lot on a Mars bar. And I got a good hiding ... never spent so much money in my life and that was tuppence.

Mrs M. commented:

> You never had any money half the week did you? By the time you paid your rent and got a bit of food in, that's it. You did

a toss up whether you had a tuppenny bar of chocolate or a quarter of tea, which was tuppence.

'We was always on the scrounge', commented one interviewee. Indeed, scrounging things such as scraps of waste sweets, wooden boxes for the copper, or pigs' heads from the butcher, seemed a permanent hobby for children. Blackberries were picked and sold to the jam factory, as were mushrooms. Petty pilfering was not beyond many of the boys:

> A few boys, including myself, used to climb the walls of Coley Goods Yard to steal bananas from Fyffes ripening shed. I think we did it because it was a treat you could only get that way.... I once called round Mr Eighteen's fishmonger's stall to steal a large kipper and when caught was smacked round the face with it, with the words, 'if you are that hungry take it'.

Poaching too, because of Coley's semi-rural position, had not died out:

> *Mr W.* Now to be quite honest lots of chaps, to supplement their food, they used to do a lot of poaching – a lot of poachers in Coley. And the ferret was a favourite animal in the house and he was kept just there, in a box, by the fire in the warm. Starved ... but kept warm. But there he was, he was their pride and joy.

Punishments for stealing could be quite severe, as this extract from the school log book shows:

> 26 May 1924:
>
> For some time sums of money have disappeared from the Headteacher's desk, and this evening the Headteacher and Mr Weeks decided to remain on the premises after the closing of the school and keep watch. At 8.30, 'X', one of our Standard VIII scholars, entered the school through a window in Room 4 and made for the Headteacher's desk. He was then captured and confessed to having taken the money from the desk on three occasions, the total amount being £3 11s 3d. His parents were then brought to the scene and instructed to take him home and keep him under strict observation 'till the morning.

On 4 June it is recorded that 'X' had been sent to a reformatory for three years.

Despite all efforts and economies many households still could not manage from one end of the week to the other, especially when children were young and unable to pay their way. Families had to resort to such measures as the 'slate' and the pawnbroker.

> *Mrs C.* Oh yes we used to have to go down and ask if we could have ... a quarter of butter or a quarter of marge ... or a half of marge and a small piece of cheese, and they used to have our name and address like, and they used to say, if you pays the weekend, you'll be able to have some more next week. But if you didn't they wouldn't let you have any more.

Mrs S.'s grandmother ran a little shop in Willow Street.

> I used to serve and they used to say, 'Give us ten Woodbines duck, and tell your gran to put it on the slate ... I'll be in on Friday'.

> *Mr A.* Mind you, they'd pay up Saturday, then they'd start again.

It was something most people tried to avoid if they possibly could.

> *Mrs M.* When I got married my brother said to me, 'Whatever you do, pay for everything as you goes along', because he was in the Co-op. He said, 'Whatever you do pay, for everything as you gets it'. Because he said, 'If you can't pay it off one week, you can't pay it off the next.' And I've been in the Co-op and they've come in and they've paid so much off last week's and so much off this week's and they're never out of debt.

There were several pawnbrokers in the area and about a third of our sample remembered the family using one, whilst the others were well aware that they were frequently used in Coley, the most used being Goodacres in the Butts and Tutty's in London Street. Often families would put the father's suit into pawn on a Monday, to be redeemed on a Saturday.

> *Mrs C.* We used to go and take perhaps a coat, one of our Fred's or our Bert's, and they used to let you have perhaps a shilling or two shillings, or something like that. Or we used to take ... perhaps ... extra bedding.

Things improved in the inter-war years. Real wages rose considerably after the First World War, and the National Insurance Act of 1911 was extended to include all groups of workers, excluding domestic servants, agricultural workers and the self-employed. The Poor Law Unions were abolished in 1929. However, for the unskilled workers of Coley the situation would have taken a great deal longer to improve than elsewhere. Unemployment, which had started to grow in the 1920s and was to become the great blight of the 1930s, was only about 6 per cent in Reading even at its peak, whereas in Jarrow it reached 67 per cent. The figures for Coley would have been somewhat different; it is a truism of a recession that the unskilled are always the first to go and although precise figures for Coley are unavailable, some indication of the level of unemployment in Coley can be gathered from this extract from the logbooks:

12 January 1922

This afternoon the treat to the children of the unemployed is being given in the Town Hall, and as a consequence our attendance is strikingly low, 184 children out of 336.

The fact that nearly half the children went does not of course mean that unemployment in Coley was nearly 50 per cent. However, it does seem reasonable to assume that it may well have been 25 to 30 per cent. And this was in 1922; it would almost certainly have risen from this. The clearances of the early 1930s would have dispersed this population so the proportion of unemployed in Coley would probably have declined after this time. It also seems that the true level of unemployment in Reading may well have been masked, as this extract from the school logbook shows:

11 January 1921

Three of our boys, who qualified by age to leave on the 23rd ult., have returned to school pending suitable employment. This had been previously recommended in view of the general unemployment in the borough.

Much of this would have been long-term unemployment. Mr A. remembered his father being out of work for years at a time, with all the subsequent effects on morale. The unemployed are remembered hanging round the streets cadging balls off the children for a game of football. The Means Test was introduced in 1931 and, with its whiff of pauperism and the old Poor Law, was much resented. Undoubtedly many of the Coley unemployed found ways of coping. John Bucknell humanely turned a blind eye to any 'moonlighting'.

> *Mr W.* They used to go, all those that were on the dole, they could go and pick spuds for him and he'd let them have time off to go and sign on the dole.

Certainly, many Coley people identified with the plight of the Jarrow marchers when they came through Reading:

> *Mr F.* Coley swimming pool, I remember that's where [they stopped] on the old Jarrow Hunger March, you know, and the Coley people, right when you come out of school, 'There you are: bread, margarine, couple of buckets of water, take them over to the men over there'.

It took the Second World War and conscription to eventually solve the unemployment problem.

The picture that emerges is one of grinding poverty for the majority of the people of Coley. A level of living where every penny was accounted for, where nothing was wasted, clothes were always second-hand, and where even with the strictest economies many families had to rely on doles and charity. The slightest misfortune could tip a family over into the abyss of increasing debt and desperation.

IV. Talking of the Coley community

'Coley appears to be a self-contained and rather self-centred neighbourhood.'
—Coley School logbook, Inspectors' report, 1 July 1923.

Coley was a separate community all of its own. There was the Co-op jam factory and Gascoignes, plus local farms and businesses for employment and the majority of goods and services could be found in the area.

Most of the shops were centred at the bottom of the Coley Steps at the junction between Coley Street, Wolseley Street and Willow Street, although there were shops strung along Wolseley Street, at the corners of the junction with Garnet Street and in Field Road and Coley Place.

Many of the 'front room' type shops were general stores but there were also boot and shoe repairers, a baker, a fish shop, a butcher and an ironmonger. One could get the services of a chimney sweep and a barber, a bookie's runner and a knife grinder.

Often these little shops provided a valuable social service. Mrs S., whose grandmother ran shop in Willow Street, recalled:

Shop in Willow Street, around 1950

> My grandmother, her shop, she used to be quite a charitable shop really ... she used to send Polly along with some groceries if they had any bad luck, if anybody was ill.

Mr D. remembers one particular shop with affection, Allens the grocers:

> What a store this was: he did coke and coal, he hired out trucks at twopence an hour. You could get firewood loose or bundled, you could buy paraffin oil, candle wax or tallow ... he sold cheese, cut meats, lard, margarine, loose jam. You name it, he sold it. Nothing was ever covered up; it was such that no Health Authority of today would allow it to exist .... One thing he always had was beer sugar; he would knock off a lump and give it to us boys for chopping a given amount of firewood. It was rather like hard caramel – to us it served as a sweet.

Field Road about 1950, showing demolition and the old fish and chip shop on the corner.

Mr W. also recalled:

> Next door [to the British Workman's Institute] was a little butcher's shop called Winifred's the Butchers, and the chap in there used to serve meat; he had a gammy hand. He always had a sock on his hand. So what was wrong you never knew, whether he cut it at some time or another, it withered or not. [The shop] was so small, if you had a side of meat up the shop was filled. And right next door to that was a fish and chip shop ... Clovers .... Now, there was a bowl of fat with a fire underneath it and he'd serve the chips, and pull the handle and the chips went through into a bucket. Now every time he pulled the handle the counter lifted in the air, really, like that. And you were leaning on it, you know, you nearly got chucked up into the air. Steam! When he put it in there, you couldn't see anywhere and it used to fill the road, everything. And the old chap used to lean right across the counter and shovel coal from across the counter, 8 foot by 9 foot was the size of the shop!

Sweet shops were remembered with particular clarity.

> *Mrs N.* [At the top of Stoney Hill], well, there was Parson's one side and Stanniford's the other side, you see ... well, Parson's was a sweet shop and we used to go and buy [sweets]; we used to make a penny last a week. We used to get an everlasting stick for a farthing, and an Allie Sloper [?], and perhaps the other farthing would buy some liquorice laces, you know, and the other was a gob stopper ... we was in heaven for a penny.

Like most shops of the time, things were sold loose and in small lots; a cup of jam, a twist of sugar. Families not only couldn't afford to buy larger quantities than this, they also didn't have the facilities for storing the food anyway.

There were also a good number of street traders who came round. There was the milkman:

> *Mr B.* Johnny Billy, he was the milkman for Johnny Bucknell's. His pony and cart [had] two milk churns either side. He used to come round with the milk [and] sell it by the pint. He came down – we had jugs then in those days – you'd come down with

Bristows, Wolseley Street, about 1965

a jug for a jug of milk. And every so often Johnny Billy'd come round with skimmed, that was a penny a pint. Oh, and for a penny a pint you could drink it, you could do such wonderful things with it too. You could make semolina cakes, all delicacies made with other skimmed milk, beautiful.

And the coalman:

Mr W. Right down the bottom of our road was the Coal Union and they always had lots of horses, you know, all horse drawn carts. Now some chaps used to have their last delivery in Wolseley Street.... And if your home was the last delivery [because in those days] they used to carry the coal right through your house and dump it, because your coal-hole was right in the back of your ... scullery, [and he'd] come out to chuck his bag on and the horse had gone, because he'd followed the other horses back to the Coal Union!

An ice cream seller from Silver Street called Mary Calangelo was known to the Coley children as Ice Cream Mary.

Mr T. My friend Ice Cream Mary, who I met every Sunday morning, and I pushed her barrow up Castle Street to Coley Place, then she gave me an ice cream and I went back to Sunday church.

There was Mr. Ming the rabbit skinner, and a muffin man who carried the muffins on a tray on his head with, apparently, the remarkable capacity of turning round whilst the tray remained stationary on his head; and there was Wally, the cat's meat man who had a shed near Rifle Range Cottages.

Mrs N. I used to go along there and play. And then you'd watch old Wally cook his horses. You could see the horses come, they used to bring the horses dead on the back of this great big cart.... Wally used to cut them up and cook [them] in a great big old pot and then slice it off, you know, and put it on skewers, and he used to come along with a great basket, covered over, and 'here comes the cat's meat man!' ... and as he come up there the cats would go and meet him, and Bobs [her cat] used to go and sit in the road and wait for him. And, of course, if we didn't get to the door to take it he used to pop it through the letterbox, and I can remember picking it up once and it looked so lovely. Lovely slices of meat, you see. He used to do about six.

For the adult population of Coley much community life centred on the pubs scattered around the streets. From the beginning of this century and onward there were five: The Borough Arms in Willow Street, the Blue Lion in Wolseley Street, the Rose and Crown and the Brickmakers, also on Wolseley Street, and the Bricklayers in Coley Place. Earlier in the century the pubs were rough, generally male establishments, and it was an unusual woman who set foot inside.

The Blue Lion

Mr Wells remembers the Blue Lion:

> [Children] used to hang round the doorway, yes. Actually, in the circumference of, outside the Blue Lion, there was always people leaning on the windowsills and against the walls, always. Always someone there. And there was a chap there would always take bets, a runner ... fights galore especially Saturday nights. And there was a little bit of spare ground that they used to fight on. Now if they couldn't settle the fight on the night – it was only gas lamps – now if they got out in the dark and you couldn't see who was who, they used to pack it in and fight over by Coley Bathing House. Start it there again Sunday mornings.

Coley, like most places, had its well-known drinkers. Mr W. writes:

> The local barber was often the subject of amusing comments. His love of the tipple was so strong that the call of the pub was often stronger than his presence in the barber's shop. Often it was that someone went in for a shave and he would not be there, so they shaved themselves and left three halfpence on the mantleshelf.

Blue Lion crowd

Drink would often be a cause of disputes in households where money was tight:

> *Mr R.* I can remember me Mum, desperately holding on to a few bob and he used to wheedle it out of her and off down the pub... he just used to wake up drunk in ditches. And in the end he went teetotal.

Mr A. writes about the Blue Lion:

> The Blue Lion was particularly renowned for being the scene of domestic violence. Angry women would congregate outside the pub on pay-day armed with hat-pins, protesting at their husbands' drinking of their wages.

However, it would not be fair to say that this was a general problem:

> *Mrs N.* Ah, but the men couldn't get the money to get drunk could they? They wasn't earning enough to get drunk on it.

Many men seem to have taken a responsible attitude and had the odd pint. They might even take the wife:

The Borough Arms, around 1965

> *Mrs C*. She might've got out, perhaps, on a Saturday down to have a glass of stout with our Dad, down – not the Blue Lion – they used to go down the Truro ... Castle Street wasn't it?

However, normally women would resort to the 'Bottle and Jug' in the early years of the century. Husbands would go out and a child might be sent with a jug to the off-licence section of a pub for a pint of stout to bring back home, or as in this instance, the husband would send the wife:

> *Mr A*. She used to get a chair, sit outside ... and she used to have this cap on. He was so deaf, he used to shout [from inside] so that everyone could hear, you know. And about quarter to ten of a night [you'd hear], 'Well the pub'll be closed, get up and get that booze gal', and she used to go walking up with her slippers and an old cap, with her jug and get the old Guinness, tuppence a pint, up the Borough Arms.

Mr W. remembered pub drinking at the beginning of the century as 'a man's thing, and women did their drinking from the Jug and Bottle, if they wanted any'.

Certainly pubs and drinking in Coley, as was the case nationally, became more respectable and open to women as the century wore on, so that by the 1930s on a typical Saturday night, according to a Mass Observation study,[68] about a third of the customers might be women.

It was to combat drunkenness in working class areas that places like the British Workman's Institute were set up. Mr A. described the interior:

> Well, you just walked in there, there was bare boards and I suppose there must have been about ten of those marble topped, old fashioned tables, and you walked straight the way down and there was an urn boiling all the time and then groceries along the top.

The British Workman's Institute amateur football team is remembered with great pride – one interviewee says it was the 'finest in the country'. It would march out to its matches with a jazz band in front and its hundreds of supporters behind.

The Church was also a centre of social life for many people. It would arrange Sunday School outings, and had its own minstrel troupe, both very popular. Carol singing at Christmas around the Steps and on Coley Avenue, crop blessing and processions were all remembered. Those that attended church mostly attended St Saviour's, but quite a number went to 'Tubb's', St Mary's Episcopal in Castle Street.

Coley was also full of its own characters, and two Coley people brought together soon get onto the topic of the colourful personalities who lived there:

> *B.M.* Whacker Barnes, he worked down the abattoir works during the day. Well, that's where I think he went. Anyway at night time he slept in the pig sties, opposite Coley Rec. And us kids, when we saw him going to work, we always asked him for a pig's bladder. Sometimes he'd bring one back for us. We used to blow this pig's bladder up like a balloon [to play football with]. That's Whacker Barnes. He used to sleep in the pig sties.

Mr Adey adds:

> Local people would give him tea when he came to the door. I seem to remember that 'Whacker' actually died in the pig sty where he slept.

'Batchy' Luker was well known locally for attending Reading's home games where, at half time, he used to run around the pitch with his dog.

> *C.W.* He also used to get a donkey and blue it with a blue bag – the donkey – so that the old donkey was blue, and sit on his back, with a stick with the old carrot in front of him, in front of the ['Drunken Seven' jazz] band. Boom, boom, and away they used to go, march, and playing the jazz band and the drum and that, all the way up to Trench Fields and all the crowd followed to support the football team.

Gypsy or Granny Smith:

> *B.M.* She lived in a cottage opposite St Saviour's Church, there was four cottages along there, and in her spare time she used to sit on the bench, in the garden. She could see right up Wolseley Street, smoking a clay pipe … oh, an old lady, yes. Gypsies, I suppose she was.

Several people remembered that when Gypsy Smith died her caravan was burnt in a traditional gypsy ceremony.

Other people are mentioned in passing. Just their names make you want know more about them, such as 'Jesus' Hood, the umbrella woman and 'Old Footsack'.

The people of Coley were fiercely insular. People from nearby communities such as Katesgrove or Castle Hill were perceived as 'foreigners', and even within Coley slight divisions existed:

> *C.W.* Now Field Road, they were a cut above us, you see. And the poor little sods in Coley, well, they were a bit rough.

One old lady who had lived in Field Road for 80 years would not be interviewed as she 'wasn't really Coley'.

Certain families lived in Coley for generations. Of our sample, out of 32 who gave information about their place of birth, 25 were born in Coley and 15 had one or both parents born in Coley. Two other people had parents who'd moved there because they already had relatives there. Nine people came from old established Coley families, going back three or four generations, some even further. No doubt, though, this is something of a self-selecting group, with only people who saw themselves as real 'Coley' people putting themselves forward to be interviewed.

Coley people did see themselves as different, mostly because few other areas suffered the extreme poverty of Coley. Coley also had a reputation for being 'rough' and this seems to have made the people defensive:

> *Mr W.* No-one had a good opinion of Coleyites. So we always said we lived 'off Berkeley Avenue' – that didn't sound so bad.

One particular Coley legend tells of a policeman, around the beginning of the century, boasting that he could 'clean up Coley' single handed. As a consequence, he was manhandled into the Holybrook, but won the respect of locals by returning to duty the following night. Whether true or not, and there is no reason to doubt it, the fact that it is retold with such amused pride says something of the feelings Coley people had for their neighbourhood.

The sense of community seems to have lingered in Coley long after it began to break up in more affluent areas.

> *Mr R.* Every house had a little wooden seat. They made one, and in the summer in the evening, everybody would sit out on their seat. You see you'd be playing, and they'd say, 'Oi! Pack it in, I shall tell your parents'.

> *Mr K.* If you were anything short, you only had to call in next door, or over the road.

Families would even take on the responsibility for looking after other children permanently if the need arose. Mr W. recalls how his father lived with his older brothers in a house in Garnet Street after his grandparents had died:

> Then my father, who was the youngest of this family – his older brothers married and gone wherever – was left with one brother in this house. And when he came home from work – every time he came home from work – something in the house had been sold. Until he had eventually come home to an empty house.

And that was it, that was it. And so he had no-one to look after him, no home, no nothing. And my (maternal) grandfather took pity on him ... and said, 'Well, poor sod, he'd better come in with us'. And that's how they, me Mum and Dad, met.

One thing that particularly drew the community together was politics, and in particular Election Day.

Mr F. One of the nicest things I used to watch then was, sort of (well because the kids don't do it now) [the] General Election. When you went and got a big poster of a candidate and nail them on the boards and then you used to go round and round, you know. 'Vote, Vote, Vote', for whoever it is, 'Chuck the other man in the sea', and all this you know.

Although the parents might have taken politics very seriously, to the children it was a glorious excuse for a game.

Mr B. Election Day in Coley was something, something I don't think you could really describe. All these hurdy-gurdies and trucks, we used to have all the placards on the side for whoever you wanted. Somehow you were convinced to vote for somebody. And once one gang leader ...

Int. That's the children or the grown ups?

Mr B. Yes the children to start with, yes. So you had your Mum's clothes post and you were like George and the Dragon, charging against the opposite numbers. Many a pitched battle was fought over – I remember in my day it was Dr Hastings, and somebody else. I forget the other one's name now, Oliver something wasn't it? And always the chant was, 'Vote, Vote, Vote for Dr Hastings. Chuck old so-and-so in the sea'. Many a mixed battle was that. And other times, of course, there was the people [who] would come round and get all you kids together, take their photographs. Give them the photo-graph – 'Now go home and tell your Mum to vote for us'.

Not surprisingly Coley was a traditional Labour voting area.

Mrs R. But oh! The Labour Party and voting day. And all the kids used to go round saying, 'Vote, vote, vote', and make their own songs.

Int. And it was all Labour?

Mrs R. Yes, it was all Labour.

Inevitably some people questioned the vast differences between their conditions and those of the 'gentry' in Coley Avenue and Castle Hill. Mr D.'s writing reflects this:

> Our Sunday School constantly reminded us that we must pray for and thank those wealthy and well-fed people who contributed items of cast-off clothing, jugs of watered-down soup and scraps left over from their tables. We were told our social position was unfortunate and that we were born to suffer…. Our only friends were our own people.

During the 1930s the Communist Party seems to have gained quite a stronghold in Reading, as it did throughout the country, and Coley was seen as fertile ground.

> *Mr M.* When Hunt, the old communist, put up, we used to have the old torchlight parades walk[ing] through Coley with all these torchlights and lumps of wood all lit and then they used to bang the old drums and they used to go over Coley, down where the waterworks place is now, and they had a hut there. And you could hear them, thumping away on the old drums. We could hear them indoors… that was lovely… we used to go out and watch them.

The councillors that people most remembered representing Coley at this time were Sam Jones, Albert Cusden and Lorenzo Quelch. Sam Jones was only the second councillor in Reading with a broadly 'socialist' platform, and by many accounts, suffered as a consequence. One of our interviewees was related to Mr Jones and said:

> He was the first Labour councillor to get paid for his duties on the Council, I believe, and he was a bricklayer and because he raked up to get things done, he was ostracised by people not giving him a job and that started him, or was the key factor in him, emigrating to New Zealand.

Lorenzo Quelch was a councillor for many years, eventually to become Alderman Quelch. He was particularly remembered for his 'very large, broad-brimmed black trilby' and Phoebe Cusden says his favourite haunt was the Rose and Crown, where he had his own special corner.

Albert Cusden was the councillor who, again according to Phoebe Cusden, was largely responsible for getting the Coley slums condemned and, ultimately, pulled down. He is remembered in Coley for a far more prosaic reason:

> *Mr W.* He had a bike that had no saddle! That's very cruel ain't it, eh? What about riding a bike with no saddle ... he had a hammock seat. It was a string thing, it had a spigot come up and a cross piece on it with holes in, and these were threaded with, like hammock cords on it, you know, and it all led to a focal point at the front ... Yes, very unkempt, typical socialist of the first water ... way back to Keir Hardie.

It would be easy to become sentimental about the community life at the time. For many people, especially before the First World War, it was an exceptionally tough and violent community, prone to erupt in fights and squabbles. The reason people called upon each other so much was simple survival; their poverty threw them together, not sociability. For a mother it was simply not possible to cook, clean, wash clothes and look after four other children just after having a baby. A neighbour's help wasn't just a nice gesture, it was absolutely vital, and nobody knew whether they might be the ones to need help next. Mr B. summed it up:

> In as much that there was something that we all shared, and that was poverty, and so no matter how bad off you were you could always rely on somebody else being worse ... brought each other together, yes. And some would be practically really dead, right down, and you'd take a little bundle of clothes that your children had grown out of and they could give to the use of their children – it's little things like that .... I think really, Reading on the whole was poor in those days. You could find many areas in Reading that were poor as well, but Coley in particular was a close-knit community, a very close-knit community.

V. Talking of growing up in Coley

'The sun always seemed to shine when I was a kid.'
—Mr W.

Most of our interviewees were really looking back to their childhood in Coley, and so one of the pictures that emerges most strongly is of the children of Coley at the time.

Of course, a dominant influence was Coley School, which as outlined earlier, was founded as a Board School after Forster's Education Act in 1870, initially in the old workhouse and then moving to purpose-built premises at the end of Coley Street in 1874.

To begin with parents resented the loss of potential income or help in the home and the somewhat high-handed approach of the school. There is a record in 1872 of some of the mothers marching on the school complaining about being asked to launder the infant girls' pinafores once a week. Mrs Thatcher, the head of the Infants at the time, agreed to ask the school board to provide a second set and the matter rested there.

An enormous emphasis was put on cleanliness. In 1899 the following Board regulation is recorded in the school log books:

> In the case of children sent to school in a dirty state or in a condition which would cause their attendance to be a discomfort or a nuisance to other children, such children may be refused admission, or if allowed to attend may (with the consent of the parent) be treated physically in such a manner as their condition may render necessary for removing or abating the cause of complaint.

However, by the early years of this century the majority of the children were attending the school spotlessly clean and relatively willingly:

> 15 June 1908. The children are neat and tidy, keen and responsive, and their general proficiency is highly satisfactory.

Children being sent home for being 'verminous' or dirty were the exception rather than the rule, and it was obviously seen as a grave slight on the mother and could cause bad feeling:

Coley School Infants, 1911

7 March 1904. On 26 February Mrs C. came to the school and used abusive and bad language. She also attempted to assault the head teacher. The latter had occasion to send her child, E, home for being dirty. The case is now in the hands of the solicitor.

Parents were expected to toe the line as much as the children; on 25 March an apology from Mrs C. was read before the school.

Punctuality, regular attendance, thrift and patriotism were also instilled in the children. Punctuality and regular attendance were enforced by the twin inducements of the cane for lateness and extra playtime for classes with 100 per cent attendance records in a week. One remarkable girl in 1910, Mabel Oke, was presented with a watch for never having missed a day in eight years.

However, the Heads had much to compete with. Attendance would fall dramatically for various Sunday school treats and the school was forced to close down on 9 February 1903 'for the visit of a menagerie to the town'. Around the beginning of the century, some families would also go hop-picking in late August:

2 September 1899. The attendance this week has been below the usual average, due to a large extent to the absence of several families in the neighbourhood who have gone hopping.

18 September 1914. A few children still away in the hop-fields.

The children could be quite ingenious in their ways of getting out of school:

> *Mr B.* I did like school, yes. Mind you, it was a wonder I ever went because I had another brother who hated school, and he's my elder brother ... he'd do anything for an excuse not to go to school. And I well remember the time, with a little spy-glass, he used to press it into my hand so hard and take me to the clinic.
>
> *Int.* To get out of going to school?
>
> *Mr B.* I had ringworm! And he had to stay behind seven days to look after me. All just because he didn't like school.

Patriotism was much encouraged. Holidays were given, for example, for the Reliefs of Mafeking and Ladysmith, for monarchs' birthdays and even the mayor's birthday. 'Theme' days were held on Trafalgar Day. Three hearty cheers were given in assembly in 1939 for the 'safe return of the King and Queen from Canada' and 24 May, Empire Day, was a half-day holiday, the first half of the day being given over to various patriotic plays, songs and marches.

> *Mr B.* On Empire Day was a day of its own and ... everybody had red, white and blue, either just a ribbon, a bow or a rosette, mainly they were all rosettes. Everybody took part in Empire Day with pride ... we all stood up and we all sang the Empire song in the assembly. That started the day off ... and these rosettes, everybody used to vie with each other, who had the best rosette, the best bows, the best anything.

Thrift was encouraged through the introduction of a penny bank, which seems to have been very well supported. On 19 December 1919, for example, when the population of the school was about 550, the penny bank had £143 9s 4d – a quite astonishing sum, indicating that, in the wealthier parts of Coley anyway, children were given pocket money to save.

Discipline was mostly enforced by the cane, which could be used for a number of offences – lateness, dirty hands, bad language, rowdy behaviour, etc. The use of the cane was regulated in November 1902 when only certain teachers were allowed to administer it. None of the women interviewed remembered being caned, although most of the men did. Girls would be kept in or made to do lines. Mrs N. recounts the following:

> When I got to 7x, there was a partition between us. There was class 7x and there was class 4 and there was a glass partition and my mind used to wander and I was always looking into class [4] and my [teacher], I can always remember him, Mr Piper. The headmaster was Mr Ellis, but Mr Piper, he always took 7x, that was the highest class. And he came out to me and said, 'Adnams, come out here.' So, of course, I thought 'What have I done now?' And he said, 'Go and open that door.' So I had to open the door of Class 4. And he said, now come back here.' And he got hold of me by the nape of the neck and he give me a push and he said, 'Now get in there,' he said, 'if you want to be in that Class 4. Your nose and eyes are always in Class 4.' He said, 'You can stay in Class 4 until you know what class you're in.' Now that was my punishment, you see.'

Parents didn't always take kindly to their children being caned. One particular incident was recounted by several people.

> *Mr W.* A lot of people used to turn up late for school, and always being told off. You see brothers used to have to bring other brothers to school and, well, they took 'em in the infants, and then came from the infants, got back and the register had been called. Well, this particular lad ... the teacher says to him, 'If you come in late again, you'll get the cane'. So, lo and behold, he comes in late again. And the kid cries and shouts and kicks, you know, and says 'I'll tell our old man of you.' And the teacher says, 'You can tell your old man of me if you like'. And the kid flew out of the door, home. So, presently, it was a very big door, like a jail door, actually, upstairs. With a clang it opens and a fellow comes in. 'Where is he, son?' he says to the lad. 'There he is.' And we were all sat there and this chap walks in ... and, Christ, when he looks at the teacher,

because the bloke's covered in blood (having come from the slaughterhouse)... and he grabs the teacher and of course the kid erupts. Hurrah! Knocks two colours out of him, that's fair enough for us you know.

The subjects taught at the school in 1913 were: Arithmetic, Reading, Composition, Spelling, Penmanship, English, Recitation, Drawing, Geography, History, Science, Music, Drill, and Needlework. Drill was a set of rigidly marshalled exercises, carried out to orders, held in the playground or school hall. It was held in the earlier years by an army sergeant, a Sergeant O'Callaghan, who eventually went off to war and was not, it seems, replaced.

Football was introduced some time after 1900 and by the late 1920s and early 1930s the school was winning trophy after trophy for football. Two boys, Luckett and Webb, became schoolboy internationals in successive years. A senior swimming trophy was won for three years and became the property of the school, as did an angling trophy. The school also did well in boxing, and numerous individuals are mentioned as having won their sections in competitions. Interviewees look back with pride on those years:

> *Mr F.* At one time there wasn't a school in Reading could beat them at anything. It was the trophies!

Some attempt was made to liven up the teaching of other subjects, with science lessons being taken down at Holybrook or over at Coley Rec, or even more adventurously:

> *Mr W.* We had a teacher named Towner and he asked the headmaster if he could get us interested in electricity ... And he used to give us this shock treatment and put a penny in the water, pick it out. You can have it if you pick it out and get a shock.

In May 1920 four senior scholars were given free flights from Woodley Aerodrome by Sir Alan Cobham. Woodwork, Metalwork and Domestic Science lessons were held over in Katesgrove School, presumably as Coley did not have the facilities.

The obvious commitment and hard work of the teachers at the school is reflected in the glowing Inspectors' Reports year after year, which talk of the staff's 'unceasing efforts', and the overall atmosphere of the school seems to have been happy.

> 29 July 1912. The older children ... are self-reliant, eager and even enthusiastic about their work.

The teachers were all too aware of the conditions that many of their pupils lived in and seem often to have paid for treats such as Christmas trees and parties themselves. The children seem generally to have been dealt with sympathetically. One inspector's report notes:

> The children are not only below the normal when they come to school, but their capacity to receive instruction is small as they soon get tired and restless.
>
> Under these circumstances the practice which obtains in the lowest class is very much to be commended; these children spend the first hour every afternoon in sleep and this practice might, with benefit, be extended to the class above ... it is noticed however that most of these children sleep on sheets of brown paper laid on the floor. This is not very comfortable especially in winter and although for sanitary reasons elaborate equipment is not desirable, something better than this could possibly be provided.

Obviously something was, as Mr F. remembers:

> They used to make you have a little sleep in the afternoons. Because I remember, and there used to be these sort of old ambulance stretchers on the floor, the big ones, and when it was washing time you had to have a little sleep on the floor.

Many of the teachers were remembered with affection – Miss Austen, Miss Hinckley, Mr Weekes, Miss Pithouse – but the two dominating personalities were Mr Ellis (Headmaster 1905–1923) and Mr Piper (Headmaster 1923–1934). Both seem to have been humane and relatively progressive. Mr Ellis records the school's first train outing – to London Zoo.

> 20 June 1921. Our venture of the 17th was a distinct success. All the 155 children appeared on the station platform and the majority of them, I am convinced, had the most interesting and comprehensive object lesson of their lives that day – 30 of them had never before been on a railway train.

However, Mr Ellis's health deteriorated rapidly and he is remembered by one as arriving at school in a taxi and hardly being able to walk. He retired in July 1923, saying:

> I write with the conviction that I have been of some little use in helping to promote the improvement in character, tone and general conditions which is so marked in the neighbourhood.

By the end of the year he was dead.

Mr Piper, who had been at the school since 1908, took over. He, too, seems possessed of some very liberal ideas, for example resisting the idea of 'holding back' slow children in a class. He writes that it is his experience that they do better if allowed to go up. Mr Piper left in 1934 to become the first headmaster at Whitley Park Junior School.

Much loyalty was built up for the school by children and parents.

> *Mr F.* I went to Coley School when I first started and when they moved up to Whitley they said. 'Oh, you'll probably have to go to Palmer School', and me and my brothers said, 'No'. And because there was no transport, or anything, so you had to walk to school and walk back at night. That was over to Whitley.

Out of school, the children led a largely outdoor life.

> *Mr B.* Us kids, we were never at home, always away, probably up Coley Rec or away somewhere, wooding, and you used to have a bottle of water and a twist of lemonade powder and that's all you needed, and a hunk of bread pudding in your pocket. And you was away for the day and you'd come back dragging plenty of wood ...

When not running errands, the children were better off out of the way of their busy mothers and they seem to have been left to their own devices from quite an early age. In the days before heavy motor traffic and when any stranger in the area would be instantly noted, this was not as careless as it may seem.

For the boys, football was a favourite pastime, although it was against the law to play it in the streets and the *Reading Chronicle* of 23 January 1930 reports that five boys were brought before the Borough Bench for 'playing football in Garnet Street' and were duly fined. Many played with a pig's bladder – probably the original 'football' – and Coley Rec was often the venue, safe from passing policemen. The girls, too, improvised their own toys.

> *Mrs S.* We used to have a celluloid doll, for a penny, and we used to have a Wills Woodbine, you know they used to have five in a packet? Used to be a big flat box they kept them in, we used to dress that up as a cradle, in them days.

The whole of Coley was a playground, from the courts and alleyways to the Holybrook, and up to 'Cundles', the allotments and beyond. The buildings themselves were part of the games.

> *Mrs I.* That used to be our rounders, the old fish shop, the wall there, we used to mark it on the fish shop wall, and we used to go to Titchmans, from Titchmans to Iremongers, from Iremongers to that relation of yours and over to the fish shop.

Some games are still familiar today – marbles, cricket, fishing, skipping with a length of rope across the road – and some less familiar:

> *Mrs N.* We always had Diabolos to play with. That's the two sticks you see and it's like a cone and you got it going in the middle, like this, you see, and once you got it going you'd throw it up and catch it.

or:

> *Mr A.* We used to have hoops, them iron hoops... and you used to run errands and that with them, miles, with a stick. These hoops, you had a little hooky thing on 'em, it caught and it kept on making it go round.

or:

> *Mr B.* Oh whip and top, it was a game you played in teams as well... you had special ways of spinning tops, you could hold the bottoms with them right up in the air and they'd go right up and come down spinning... The most popular top of all, there was the mushroom top. And the mushroom top, it was about the size I'd say of a fair size mushroom. And you always coloured it. Bits of chalk, you always made little

designs, so that when it was spinning it looked lovely. But with a mushroom, you would hit it and it would go for miles. And after that came a larger one called a window breaker, because it was an unsteady top, and once you hit it, instead of going straight up like a mushroom top would, a window breaker would swerve either side and typically did break a lot of windows ... After that came the turnip, like a turnip, flat at the top and going narrow right down to the bottom. Little turnip top ... that was a girl's top ... as I say, you could hit the old mushroom ... up the street and other people'd hit it back and then you'd gang up, two a side probably ... Oh it used to be wonderful fun.

Another popular game, a variant of 'Hide and Seek', was called 'Erky Erky' – a game still played, and now often called 'Kick the Can'.

> *Mr W.* We used to get on a manhole cover and they all used to run and hide, you know. And then they would have to come and find you. If he could see you first he had to run back and bang that quick to catch you out. But if you got back to that manhole cover before him, you were still in.

As another said:

> *Mr B.* We knew all the nooks and crannies in Coley and we used to play 'Erky Erky 1, 2, 3' and we'd hide from everything everywhere ... there was many a canoodling done in that ... From that 'Erky Erky' we found out things that birds and bees never do.

Naturally they enjoyed their practical jokes as much as children ever have done:

> *B.M.* Release and tying the knockers up, with a bit of string all along the street. As one opened the door, that one she shut her door. The other one banged didn't it ... And they used to tie all the string on the letter boxes.

> *I.M.* We use to play the policemen up as well.

> *B.M.* Have a shoebox on a piece of string and you used to put it out on the pavement and when somebody come along, we used to pull it along so's they couldn't touch. Anyway, a copper

came along one day and caught us. I think the policemen was frightened to come round our way in those days.

A popular place for playing was the swimming baths – 'a proper little lido' as it was described. Where the Holybrook actually ran through Coley, then, as now, it was protected by railings, although some of these were easily removed. Further out, behind Rifle Range Cottages, the river was different – deeper and cleaner.

B.D. It being sparkling and clean, one could always see the gravel bottom and shoals of minnows and dace.

Mr A. remembered:

We used to go fishing, but there used to be an old bridge there and when you went over that bridge to Rifle Range Cottages you went over that little old bridge. The gates were nearly always locked but you could squeeze through, and turn left and there was a little sluice gate that led into the Kennet and we used to play there. Opening, no we didn't used to open it but we used to play with the water there, like, you know. Used to spend hours over there.

Fishing was enormously popular, although tackle was basic:

R.F. One of my little sports was getting a line, and one or two little shops in Coley sold fishing hooks, because it was near the River Kennet. You got a penny hook and tied it on the line, put a bit of bread on and dangle it down the wall and take a chance that somebody'd come and push you in or anything. You know … lay down there and dangled it down the side and the gudgeon used to come along in shoals … And I always used to wonder if, when I see these men with these big fishing rods, I always think, well one day I hope I can get something like that, which I did.

The proximity of the rivers may well explain the Coley children's proficiency in both swimming and fishing, although it did have its dangers. The Coley School Log Book records 'whilst playing 10/7/1908 George Plested drowned'.

Many games were by their very nature seasonal, such as swimming, cricket, football, conkers and winter games:

I.M. I remember when the snow was on the ground, all the kids used to come on little trays down [Stoney or Garnet Hill]. One used to stand at the bottom to see if it was all right – there wasn't many cars about then – and they'd come straight down the hill ... and some of them went nearly down the Brook, didn't they?

B.M. Some of them used to finish up in the shop.

As children reached their teens or even older the streets were still the main meeting place, hanging about under the gas lights or playing cards in the little alleys and courtyards:

Mr B. The most used and abused being the Box Tunnel, here in hidden corners many a game of cards were played. Ask any Old Coleyite what the Box Tunnel Shuffle was and they'll tell you ... these games were only played for half pennies and pennies but there was more urgency to win than any game played at Monte Carlo.

The old cliché that children made their own fun in those days seems particularly appropriate to Coley, but then Coley, with its steep hill and little alleyways, its rivers, fields and its open community, was a natural playground. A frequent comment was that these people never really remembered being bored; in fact, there were not enough hours in the day:

Our mums would come out and call us and we used to say 'just another ten minutes, just another few minutes' then our dads used to call and we knew we had to go in then.

VI. Talking of health, medicine, illness and death

> 'When one looks more closely at, for instance, the children in the two lowest classes it is noticed that for many of them the home conditions must be adverse both physically and mentally. In one of these classes the majority of children were either anaemic in appearance or undersized, or had other evidence of poor physical condition ...'
> —Inspector's Report: Coley School, October 1923.

Growing up in the poorer districts of any town in the early years of this century was a hazardous business, and Coley was no exception. Being born and surviving infancy was the first hurdle; the infant mortality rate in 1900 was 140 deaths for every 1000 births. Since families of nine or ten children were still quite common in Coley at this time, and the infant mortality rate higher the poorer you were, most families in this area could expect to lose at least one baby in the family in the opening years of this century.

Roughly a quarter of our sample remembered stillbirths or infants dying in the family; these were mainly the older interviewees from the worst housing. The most dramatic example was a family of 16 births where only 11 survived. There was precious little ceremony to mark the passing of some of these children.

> *Mrs S.* My own father, of the two we had die in our family, he ... made the coffin for this little baby and dressed it and put it in the coffin and strapped it on the back of his bike and took it up to the Henley Road Cemetery ... Mum had the number of it ... say there was an open grave that day they dropped that down but you have the number of the grave.

This particular baby was a breech delivery, at home with nobody but a local woman to assist. At this time most women only had a local experienced woman to help them. Local authorities were not obliged to provide midwives until 1936, although there was some limited provision before then. All births were at home.

Although it has been difficult to gather much direct evidence of this in Coley, studies done elsewhere it the country at this time

(1900–1920) show that women would usually get the worst of the food, even while pregnant, and were actually advised in some cases to starve themselves in the last month of pregnancy to make the baby smaller and hence the birth easier. Mothers would be back on their feet after a day or so as families could not afford the luxury of them lying in, although neighbours and relatives would often help out. Other children in the family seem almost to have been taken by surprise by a birth.

> *Mr M.* I remember the last ... I saw her in the garden, before I went to school lunchtime, hanging up the clothes and when I got back from school ... in the afternoon she was in bed with the baby ... I can see our Mum now, she was cutting the bread up ... for our lunch, and she said, 'When you comes home I'll be in bed with the baby.' So of course when we gets home, we couldn't find her and we said 'Where's Mum? Where's Mum gone?'

Local amateur 'midwives' could build up quite a reputation for themselves:

> *Mr T.* Mrs Coles that used to live down the terrace, she was – it was one of the reasons why I never left this house, because I had such faith in her. We had three children, she brought them all into the world. None of them went to hospital. It was all done up in the bedroom you know.

For women having their second, third or more child, with no complications and a clean house, the environment was as suitable, if not more so, than any they could get in a hospital at the time.

Almost all women breast-fed their babies for convenience and cheapness, and as a consequence probably protected their children from many of the infections from poorly sterilised bottles that children of wealthier, bottle-feeding parents might be prone to. Formula milk was too expensive, so if a mother could not breast feed, children could be put on to cow's milk, or a 'farinaceous' mixture of flour and water..

Normal childhood illnesses took their toll – measles, whooping cough, scarlet fever, chickenpox and diphtheria. At the beginning of the century by far the biggest killers were measles and whooping cough. These were responsible for 917 and 815 deaths per million children under 15 respectively in the first decade of this century, although again this figure would have been a great deal higher in the poorer districts. A measles epidemic at Coley School, as at all council schools, was taken very seriously. An outbreak of measles in a family had to be reported to the school, who would exclude the child for four weeks:

> 21 June. Received notification from the Medical Officer of the prevalence of measles in the homes of the following – exclusion to extend for four weeks from the date appended,
>
> | | |
> |---|---|
> | 2 Katesgrove Lane | June 1st |
> | 6 Fir Court | June 13th |
> | Wolseley Street | June 13th |
> | 18 Bosier Street | June 14th |
> | 30 Coley Street | June 14th |
> | 1 Weston Terrace | June 16th |

The following week there were ten more notifications, but very soon after the situation deteriorated rapidly, as on 4 July the Urban Sanitary Authority of Reading ordered the closure of the school for four weeks. The summer holidays started on 26 July that year and finished on 25 August, but the measles epidemic seems to have raged all summer, as an entry for 26 August ordered the school to remain closed for another four weeks. It opened again on 10 September with an attendance of 147 out of 200, three fresh notifications of measles and three of scarlet fever. The exclusion period for scarlet fever was six weeks, and for diphtheria two weeks.

The twin factors of inadequate diet in the poorer areas and overcrowding meant that diseases spread rapidly and were far more serious. Mr D. remembers:

> a number of my little friends died early through one or other of these diseases that were so common to us.

Influenza too, could be quite a serious illness, but no outbreak more serious than the notorious epidemic of Spanish 'Flu in 1918–1919 that caused 150,000 deaths in England and Wales and 15 million worldwide. The epidemic first reached England in late spring 1918. On 5 July 1918 the log books record:

> Over a hundred children have been attacked by what is known as Spanish Influenza ... the school will be closed for one week.

The school re-opened on 15 July, with the epidemic apparently on the wane. However, by 23 October it had reappeared and this time seems to have taken a more widespread hold:

> The school will close this afternoon until 5 November owing to the prevalence of influenza among the staff and scholars of this town.

It does not in fact reopen until 25 November. The epidemic appeared again in February 1919, but this time did not close the school. Mrs N. remembers:

> The only thing I can remember is 1919, and that's when they had the 'flu epidemic after the war. Well my father was very ill with influenza and I had it. I had a bed up in the corner and he had the other bed. And I can remember there was a military funeral was going to come into the church and ... I could hear this band coming along you see, playing the Dead March, and I got out of bed to look and the next thing I know I'm on the floor in a dead faint. And I can remember my mother saying 'George, I'm sure she's dead, I'm sure she's dead. Get the doctor, I'm sure she's dead'.

The number of deaths from childhood illnesses declined rapidly up until the Second World War, deaths from measles declining most rapidly to 217 per million children under 15 in 1938. Diphtheria, however, does not seem to have declined at anywhere near the rate of the others and was the deadliest childhood disease of all by 1938; the school records two serious outbreaks that year and two deaths that winter.

> *Mr A.* I can remember four or five dying of diphtheria, we had just before the war, a diphtheria epidemic.

> *Mrs S.* Yes, I remember that. And when whoever it was died, they used to send somebody along from the council and they used to fumigate the house all out, didn't they, spraying it and things.

Amongst the general population, however, the disease responsible for more deaths than all the others put together in the first half of this century was tuberculosis, known as TB or consumption. In 1910 alone, 51,000 people died of the disease, and although this had almost halved to 27,000 by 1940, it was still a substantial killer. Mrs N. remembers her 28-year-old sister:

> *Mrs C.* She died of what they used to call consumption.
>
> *Mrs N.* That's right yes, TB.
>
> *Int.* And was that before the Second World War?
>
> *Mrs N.* That was, yes ... I used to go and see her when she was at home. She used to come in here for a day and she used to have a terrible cough.

The only 'cure' of the time was rest, sunlight and fresh air – not things to be found in abundance in the slum areas of Coley.

> *Mrs S.* It used to be terrible, didn't it; they used to have them out in the garden, didn't they?
>
> *Int.* Did they? What, to sleep?
>
> *Mrs E.* Yes, yes. They used to have a shed at the bottom of the garden, most people, didn't they? If they really had TB.

But once caught, there was no reliable cure:

> *Mr G.* Yes it was always fatal, TB was.
>
> *Mr K.* Nine times out of ten I think. You see our mothers used to whisper in those days 'consumption' she used to say then. It was always taboo for some reason or other.

The disease continued to cast its shadow long after it had declined as a real threat.

> *Mrs R.* (talking of the late fifties): [mum] always used to say to us 'Now look, if you get tired you'll end up with TB'. That was always her fear when we was teenagers because it used to happen to them you know.

The government had been so concerned about the physical state of the recruits for the Boer War that they set up the Interdepartmental Committee on the Health and Physique of the Population. As a result of its recommendations several measures were passed. One was the Education (Provision of Meals) Act of 1906. In 1905 the Reading Education Committee made enquiries about seriously underfed pupils and Coley School returned six names; their addresses read like a catalogue of the slums: Castle Hill Place, Rose Court, Bosier Square, Commercial Hall, Box Court and Somerset Place. On 12 December 1905 free breakfasts were provided for needy pupils, served at The British Workmen's Hall six days a week. Ninety children qualified for this out of 180. These breakfasts were, however, discontinued in 1909. More permanently, the Southampton Street Feeding Centre was opened in 1906 in response to government legislation. This provided free school meals for needy Reading children; about 30–40 Coley children used to attend at this time. There can be little doubt that access to free school meals had a major influence on the general health of children from poor homes, affecting not only their weight and height but also their ability to resist disease.

The Public Health Amendment Act of 1907 set up the School Medical Service and the first medicals were held at Coley School in 1908. From then on regular medical and dental examinations of the children took place, a certain Dr Taylor doing the inspections for many years. There were also the more routine 'Nitty Nora' inspections for head lice. Children who attended the Southampton Street Feeding Centre had their weight and height closely monitored.

Beyond this, medical care was more patchy. From 1913 most workers who paid their stamps were entitled to some sort of free medical care, and by 1928 this had extended to 15 million workers nationwide. Their dependents were not, however, entitled to go up 'before the panel' and for those who could manage it, money was paid into some sort of sick club or health insurance scheme.

> *Mr F.* My mum used to pay a penny a week into the Royal Berkshire Hospital Scheme and you could be an inmate and have an operation for that.

The People's Dispensary ran a similar scheme for medicines, although the poorest could get them free.

Mrs C. And there was a dispensary then that run from the back of Heelas.

Mrs N. Oh that's right, yes, we used to go and collect medicines from there.

Mrs C. They used to find out, you know, how you were sort of managing... if you had free meals and that, you usually got free medicines. But mums and dads had to sign the paper and the oldest one had to go and fetch it round the dispensary.

Otherwise, medical charges could be ruinous:

Mrs R. My dad, in the war, he was in the Fleet Air Arm and one of the ships he was on they had smallpox on board... Everybody had to be cabled... 'Make sure your families vaccinated against smallpox.' My Mum didn't like doctors and I was such a bad-tempered baby... so she didn't have it done. So when my Dad came home he went mad... (he) got in touch with the (doctor) and he come out and vaccinated me and my Mum. My dad got a fiver out of his pocket and said to him, 'How much is that?' and he said, 'That'll do nicely' and put it in his pocket.

Unsurprisingly, many people would rely on their own cures or those of local experts, such as one man in Brook Street:

Mrs R. He belonged to the Red Cross. He used to do things and my mum said she can remember having an enormous great boil, I think it was on her arm... She said 'I can remember him lancing my boil'... It was the first time she nearly fainted and it was the only thing.

The home-made cures ranged from the mildly pleasant – liquorice, boiled onions, syrup of figs – to the frankly disgusting – goose-grease, brimstone and treacle, castor oil and camphorated oil, sulphur tablets and Russian Tallow.

Mrs M. When you had a cold when we was kids, our mother used to cut out a brown heart out of paper and put tallow on it, tallow candle, and put it all over that and stuck that on your chest and you had that on for two or three days. And it used to do your chest good.

Or,

> If you had a sore throat, somebody's sweaty sock, you put that round your neck when you went to bed.

It would be wrong to give the impression that the population of Coley was completely disease-ridden. Undoubtedly, the poorest children were undernourished in the first few decades but by 1925 attendances at the Southampton Street Feeding Centre had dropped to eight. Many infants and children died, but also many people couldn't remember having a day's illness in their lives. The children for the most part seem to have led a hardy, outdoor life with basic but nourishing food. Coley School won boxing, football and swimming trophies year after year in the 1920s and 1930s. There is no doubt that standards of health improved dramatically at this time. More than two-thirds of conscripts in the First World War were unfit for duty; less than one third were by the Second. Infant mortality dropped from 142 to 31.2 per 1000 by 1950. There can be little doubt that the nationwide slum clearances of the 1920s and 1930s, of which the clearances in Coley were a small part, were a major factor in reducing infection and disease amongst the poorest. Diseases such as diphtheria and tuberculosis went into decline years before the inoculations were developed. Perhaps ironically the rationing of the Second World War improved the diet of the poor, ensuring a good balance of proteins and vitamins at low prices. The National Health Service Act of 1946, providing free health care 'from the cradle to the grave', did much to ensure that one did not come quite so soon after the other. For women, improved access to family planning techniques ensured fewer pregnancies, and the NHS took better care of both mother and baby.

This small revolution was reflected in Coley, where funerals became less of a common sight and sawdust strewn on the road to muffle noises outside the houses of the sick a thing of the past. Mrs R.'s brother died of bronchial pneumonia, aged six weeks, after the Second World War. A wreath was collected for and 153 people signed the sheet of paper in the local shop. Compared to the breech birth at the beginning of this chapter 'it was quite a rare thing and it touched everyone'.

VII. Coley moves on

Clearance, the war and redevelopment 1930–1970

Councillors such as Jones, Rabson and Connelly had repeatedly raised the issue of slum housing in the opening years of the century, but as a minority their power was limited. It was a later generation, with the long-standing Quelch and Albert Cusden in the 1930s, that were to see their ambitions realized.

The Council did not seriously get round to tackling the issue of insanitary and inadequate housing until 1917, when a Housing and Town Planning Committee was established.[69] A site for 600 houses was identified at Manor Farm, but there was considerable opposition from the Labour Party locally, who said it was too near the sewage works and on low-lying damp land.[70] Further sites were later identified in Norcot and off the Shinfield Road in Whitley. Dr Ashby, the Medical Officer of Health, identified 330 houses in Reading as unfit for human habitation in 1919; most of them were in Coley. Progress was slow, however, with political changes and a weakened economy at national level impeding building as finance regimes changed from municipal to private.

Fresh impetus was given by the 1930 'Greenwood' Housing Act, which gave wide powers and responsibilities to local authorities. The first slum clearance order appeared on 5 October 1931 and targeted Coley. It is noticeable that the next three also focused on Coley. It was obviously seen as the most pressing of problems for the Corporation.[71] Landlords of these properties continued to resist their demolition to the very end. The Darvall Brothers, local bakers, and also landlords in the Coley clearance area, gave evidence to an inquiry that their properties should be spared as they could make good any repairs, and the fact that windows could not be opened was actually a security feature.[72] The Council won the appeal, however. By April 1932 48 families had been moved out.[73]

The waiting list for new houses was long, with 3,000 applicants by 1925. Only 99 families from Coley and Silver Street had been rehoused by the end of 1934. Some of the lag came from a reluctance to move elderly residents, who were loath to move from everything they had ever known. Dr Milligan, the Medical Officer of Health in 1934, said:

It would be a doubtful kindness to uproot these people and remove them to new surroundings far from associations which have been the major part of their lives.[74]

Many found the new council house rents unacceptably high. Rules governing behaviour were tight: gardens had to be well-maintained, furniture considered verminous could not be brought, the houses could not be wallpapered without the permission of the Council, animals and poultry could not be kept, council workmen had the right to enter the house 'at all reasonable hours of the day' to carry out maintenance work, sheds could not be built in the gardens.

Even so, the luxury of a toilet, not only *not* shared with other households, but actually inside the house, must have seemed tremendous. In addition, houses were supplied with fixed baths and hot and cold running water, there were wardrobes in the bedrooms, and gas fires upstairs and down. Although the old communities were broken up, many found themselves neighbours to other Coleyites on the Whitley streets.[75]

By 1935 large areas of Coley were cleared, and the Corporation was then left with the problem of the empty land. It was still owned by the small landlords who had owned the houses, a patchwork quilt of smallholdings. The Corporation's great fear was that more tenements and commercial premises would start to spring up on the land, so in 1935 they decided to compulsory-purchase the land to prevent this.

The Corporation were challenged about what they would do with the land, their reply being that 'until required for housing and other purposes the land (will) be retained as open space'. Eighty-five years later, much of the land still is.

By 1939 Reading Council had 3,140 houses on its books, and the clearance of the worst slums of Coley was almost complete. The Second World War put a stop to much of this, and the community of Coley was sufficiently intact to respond to the challenges of war.

At 5.10 on the morning of 3 October 1940, three small bombs were dropped on Coley, one falling just by St Saviour's Church. Fortunately, there were no fatalities, apart from the milkman's horse, out on the morning round.[76]

VE Day, May 1945, Garnet Street, with two American GIs

As with most populations, Coley lost many of its men, and the women would have struggled to feed their families as much as anywhere else.

Like many communities, Coley joined in the celebrations at the end of the War.

The post-war years may have seemed like some sort of golden age for Coley, with the worst of the slums gone but much of the community infrastructure intact. The Blue Lion, the Borough Arms, the Rose and Crown and the Bricklayers Arms were still open for business. There was a Boys' Club and plenty of little grocers, hardware stores and even a fish and chip shop. It became a thriving, solid, healthy place to live. It can be seen as a little microcosm of the transformation that slum clearance, the NHS, state education and the welfare state effected on British society in the mid-20th century.

A map of 1957 shows courts and passages gone, as well as much of Coley Street, but Henrietta Street, Parnell Street and Bright Street were still there and the link straight on to Castle Street still exists.

One of the last pictures of Coley Street, before demolition, looking up towards Castle Street.

The population of Coley in the 1950s and 1960s would have stood at about 2000, and many families had been there for generations. There was still work locally, at the jam factory and Gascoignes on Berkeley Avenue, and at the garages and shops around Coley and Castle Street.

However, Reading was not standing still, and in the 1960s and 1970s its economy was shifting rapidly from blue-collar production, brewing and biscuits to white-collar office work, insurance, IT and public sector work. The demands of the motorcar were becoming more insistent. The jam factory closed in 1968, and Gascoignes at about the same time.

Slum clearances around nearby Hosier Street and Grape Passage had left great areas of the centre open for redevelopment. The Borough Council had recognised soon after the war that they would need new administrative offices, as the site on Friar Street which had served the authority since the late 18th century was simply too small. By 1959, both political groups had accepted this and broadly agreed on the Hosier Street site, which opened as the Civic Offices, the Hexagon and the Police Station in the mid-1970s.[77] The M4 opened in 1971, taking a great deal of through traffic away from Reading. The local authority decided to improve the passage of traffic through the centre with an 'inner-city motorway', which would act as internal ring road, with exits to key points in the town. The Inner Distribution Road (IDR) was started in the late 1960s and the first part opened in 1969. This involved the final bulldozing of Coley Street, and the last pubs and shops it contained, as well as the removal of Henrietta Street, Bright Street and Parnell Street.

The Coley Branch line finally closed in 1981.

Postscript: Old Coley now

The IDR did a very good job of cutting Coley off from the town centre. Field Road and Coley Place still enter onto Castle Street, but Wolseley Street now faces a four-lane motorway between it and the town. New developments in the 1970s and 1980s, such as new council flats in Coley Place and private developments in St Paul's Court, Cheriton Court, Pennyroyal Court and later Ruby and Opal Courts off Lower Field Road, kept the population up. 'Courts' have returned to Coley, but in a completely different form. However, the little shops in and around Field Road and Wolseley Street are all gone. Somerville Glass, still open when the first *Talking of Coley* books were written in 1989, has now also gone. Now Berkeley Stores and the garage on Berkeley Avenue serve the area, and a little local bakery has recently opened on Wolseley Street. The Castle Tap, a reinvention of the Horse and Jockey on Castle Street, has recently woken up to start serving the

Castle Tap, Castle Street

local community again, and at the time of writing, the hopes of all in these streets is that it will survive the coronavirus lockdown.

The school continues and thrives, with 290 children aged 3–11 on the roll and 40 different languages spoken by the pupils. St Saviour's Church, built to replace the old iron church on the playground, is still there, now the evangelical All Nations Christian Centre, and the church hall is a drop-in centre for the homeless. The Salvation Army, again evicted from their home in St Mary's Butts for the new civic offices and shopping centre, were given land made available after clearance off the old Coley Street and Willow Street, and built a new homeless hostel called 'Willow House', which opened around 1970. It occupies a site not only yards from where they had begun in Reading nearly 100 years before, but also close to that of the old workhouse, Coley Hall, in which they had had to take refuge from the hostile crowds of Coley.

On 5 January 2000 two houses in Field Road collapsed dramatically into a sink hole, causing a power cut to the entire area. On

Subsidence from the old chalk mines in the 1950s. A problem eventually tackled in 2000.

investigation other, smaller, unexplained incidents of subsidence in the road over the years now fitted into a pattern. The old brick kilns, which had used mined chalk in the production of bricks, had left their legacy. On investigation, chalk mines were found to snake under the road for hundreds of yards.

Reading Borough Council and English Heritage spent the next five years backfilling and underpinning the whole street to compensate for the industrial legacy of 150 years before.

The streets around Garnet Hill and Garnet Street still carry hints of the past in old walls and cobblestones. The well-built 'cottages' that 'Squire' Monck so proudly showed to the Rev. Crawfurd on a hot day in 1887 are still family homes. The steep slope where the Steps once housed a whole community is now trees and bushes, overshadowed by a footpath over the IDR. Nowadays there are more cars parked up along the streets, and a small play area serves the current generation of children, a quiet handful compared to the very many over two hundred years who played in the courts, yards and alleyways of Old Coley.

Endnotes

I. Pigney's Lane

1. Speed's 1611 map does show one building on the Holybrook. This may be indicative of a larger community, but it is not certain.
2. Harman, L. *History of Christianity in Reading* (Reading: Bradley and Son, 1952) p. 55.
3. Chaucer, *The Millers Tale* (Project Gutenberg), line 3269.
4. For similar, and more graphic, name-evolution see Grape Lane in York. Joan Dils notes a Grope Lane in pre-1350 Reading, at modern day Chain Street, suggesting the 'zone' had moved out of the centre as the town developed.
5. BRO D/EX37/T/2.
6. BRO D/ECd T12/14 *Summary of land holdings for the Coley Estate.*
7. *Ibid.*
8. BRO D/P 98 28/19 *Residents of St Mary's Parish* 1783.
9. BRO D/ECd T12/14.
10. Simons, M. *Housing the Working Classes of Reading 1837–1939* (PhD thesis, unpublished, 2007) p. 36.
11. *Ibid*, p. 33.
12. *Ibid*, p. 26.
13. Blake, S. T. *The Physical Expansion of the Borough of Reading, 1800–1862* (Reading: University of Reading, 1976) p. 62.
14. Anon. *A correct list of the voters at the Election of the Two Burgesses to serve in Parliament for the Borough of Reading* (Reading: Drysdale, 1826) p. 13.
15. *Ibid*, p. 248.
16. Blake, *The Physical Expansion*, p. 253.
17. Simons, *Housing the Working Classes*, p. 324.
18. 1841 census, excluding the workhouse, but including Coley Kiln Cottages.
19. Blake, *The Physical Expansion*, p. 117.
20. Crawfurd, Rev. G. P. *Recollections of St Mary's Reading, 50 years ago* (Reading: Morley, 1932)
21. RM 10/7/1875.
22. BRO D/EX 119/7 Monck family papers.
23. *Report of the Medical Officer of Health for the Urban Sanitary Authority of Reading* (MOH Report) 1883.
24. Sherman, Rev. J. *The Pastor's Wife* (New York: American Tract Society, 1850). Sherman referred to Coley-lane, which is modern day Coley Avenue, confusing it with Coley-street, which Hanover Square came off. He was only in Reading a few years, and wrote this many years later.
25. Billing, J. Statistics of the Sanitary Condition of the Borough of Reading, *Journal of the Statistical Society of London*, 10(3) (Sep 1847) p. 259–261.
26. *Reading Mercury*, Sat 24 February 1847.
27. Inspector's Reports 6th July 1865.
28. *Berkshire Chronicle* 8 Oct 1870.
29. MOH Report, 1885.
30. MOH Report, 1882.
31. Simons, M. *Housing the Working Classes*, p. 242.

32 See, for example, Reid, A. Infant feeding and child health and survival in Derbyshire in the early 20th century, *Women's Studies International Forum*, 60, p. 111–119.
33 Although Childs states a 'silk factory' operated near St Laurence's church at this time, it can only have been a small business. Childs, W. *The Town of Reading at the beginning of the nineteenth century* (Reading: University College, 1910) p. 13.
34 Jones, S. R. H. Technology, Transaction Costs and the Transition to Factory Production in the British Silk Industry, 1700–1870. *The Journal of Economic History*, 47(1) (Mar 1987) p. 71–96.
35 HoC. *Report from Committee on Silk Ribbon Weavers Petitions*, 3 June 1818. p. 156.
36 *Reading Mercury*, 27 April 1829.
37 https://berkshireresearch.wordpress.com/2014/04/18/berkshire-silk-weaving/
38 BRO D/N 9/14/2 *Report read at the opening of the Coley Schools*.
39 Bowley, A. L. and Burnett-Hurst, A. B. *Livelihood and Poverty A study in the Economic Conditions of Working Class Households in Northampton, Warrington, Stanley and Reading* (London: Bell and Sons, 1915) p. 173.
40 BRO D/P 98 8/4 VM Apr 1772.
41 Eden, F: *The State of the Poor* Vol. 2 (Gale Ecco, 1795) p. 11.
42 Darter, W. S. *Reminiscences of Reading: By an octogenarian* (Reading: Blagrave Street Steam Printing Works, 1889) p.110.
43 BC 12/2/1870.
44 BRO D/N 9/14/2.
45 BC 7/10/1871.
46 *Ibid*.
47 BC 12/2/1870.
48 BC 7/10/1871.
49 BRO/89/SCH/48/3, Coley School Log Books (Boys/Girls/Infants) 19/1/1872.
50 Logbooks Jan 1873.
51 Cusden, P. *Portrait of an Urban Village* (WEA Reading, 1977) p. 18.
52 RO 18/7/1874.
53 Mitford, Mary Russell. *Belford Regis: or Sketches of a country town* (Bentley, London, 1846) p. 355.
54 RM 13/10/1861.
55 RM 8/11/1902 and RO 6/11/1902.
56 RO 16/10/1920.
57 RO 10/12/1881.
58 RM 8/6/87.
59 RM 30/01/1904.
60 BRO *A correct list of voters 1826*.
61 Taken from 1919 Electoral Register, Minster Ward minus non-Coley streets such as Gun Street, Bridge Street etc approximate to allow for some author error.
62 Guilding, *Diary of the Corporation of Reading 1431–1602*, Vol 1 (Parker, 1892) p. 10.
63 Blondel, J. The Conservative Association and Labour Party in Reading, *Political Studies* (1959, Vol 6) p. 101–119, p. 111.
64 RO 17/11/1917.
65 *Reading Observer*, 28 May 1910.

III. Talking of making ends meet

66　Hylton, S. *Reading, 1800 to the Present Day. The Making of Modern Reading Day* (Stroud: Amberley, 2015) p. 137.
67　*Reading Observer*, 19 Feb 1921.

IV. Talking of the Coley community

68　Harrison, T. & Madge C. *Britain by Mass Observation* (London: Century Hutchison, 1986).

VII. Coley moves on

69　Alexander, A. *Borough Government and Politics* (Allen and Unwin, 1985) p. 196.
70　Simons, *Housing the Working Classes*, p. 251.
71　*Ibid*, p. 270.
72　BC 1/1/1932, in Clapson, M, *Working Class Suburb, Social Change on an English Council Estate, 1920-2010* (Manchester University Press, 2012) p. 34.
73　*Ibid*, p. 35.
74　Simons, *Housing the Working Classes*, p. 278.
75　Clapson, *Working Class Suburb,* p. 52.
76　Cooper, M. *Early Closing Day: Air Raids on Reading 1939-1945* (Reading: Scallop Shell Press, 2016) p. 72.
77　Alexander, *Borough Government,* p. 216.

Bibliography

Adams, C. *Ordinary Lives* (London: Virago) 1982

Alexander, A. *Borough Government and Politics* (Allen and Unwin) 1985

Aspinall, A. et al. *Parliament through Seven Centuries and its MPs* (Hansard) 1962

Bowley, A. L. and Burnett-Hurst, A. R. *Livelihood and Poverty: A study in the Economic Conditions of Working-Class Households in Northampton, Warrington, Stanley and Reading* (Bell and Sons) 1915

Bowley, A. L. and Hogg, M. H. *Has poverty diminished?* (Bell and Sons) 1924

Chaucer, G. *The Canterbury Tales* (Penguin Classics) 2003

Clapson, M. *Working Class Suburb, Social Change on an English Council Estate, 1920–2010* (Manchester University Press) 2012

Cooper, M. *Early Closing Day: Air Raids on Reading 1939–1945* (Reading: Scallop Shell Press) 2016

Crawfurd, Rev. G. P. *Recollections of St Mary's Reading, 50 Years Ago* (Reading: Morley) 1932

Cusden, P. *Portrait of an Urban Village* (Reading: WEA) 1977

Darter, W. S. *Reminiscences of Reading: By an octogenarian* 1889

Dils, J. *Reading: A History* (Carnegie) 2019

Eden, F. *The State of the Poor, Vol 2* (Gale Ecco) 1795

Guilding, Rev. J. M. *Diary of the Corporation of Reading* (Parker) 1892

Harman, L. *History of Christianity in Reading* (Reading: Bradley and Son) 1952

Hylton, S. *Reading, 1800 to the Present Day. The making of modern Reading* (Stroud: Amberley) 2015

Lynch, G. *History of Gauged Brickwork* (Amsterdam: Butterworth-Heinneman) 2007

Madge, C. *Britain by Mass Observation* (London: Century Hutchinson Ltd) 1986

Pember-Reeves, M. *Round about a pound a week* (London: Virago) 1979

Quelch, L. *An Old-fashioned Socialist* (Reading: Kempress) 1992

Railton, M. and Barr, M. *Battle Workhouse and Hospital* (Reading: Berkshire Medical Heritage Centre) 2005

Roberts, R. *The Classic Slum* (Manchester University Press) 1971

Sherman, Rev. J. *The Pastor's Wife* (American Tract Society) 1850

Smith, B. *The Boathouse Corps: The Story of the Salvation Army in its First Year in Reading* (Self-published) 2014

Articles

Billing, J. 'Statistics of the Sanitary Condition of the Borough of Reading.' *Journal of the Statistical Society of London*, 10(3) (Sep. 1847) 259–261

Blondel, J. 'The Conservative Association and Labour Party in Reading.' *Political Studies*, 6 (1959) 101–119

Jones, S. R. H. 'Technology, Transaction Costs and the Transition to Factory Production in the British Silk Industry, 1700–1870'. *The Journal of Economic History*, 47(1) (Mar 1987)

McCormack, A. 'The Irish in Nineteenth Century Reading'. *Berkshire Old and New*, 27 (2010) 27–47

Reid, A. 'Infant feeding and child health and survival in Derbyshire in the early twentieth century'. *Women's Studies International Forum*, 60 (2017) 111–119

Unpublished PhD theses

Blake, S. T. 'The Physical Expansion of the Borough of Reading, 1800–1862' (University of Reading, 1976)

Cook, A. 'Reading, 1835–1930: A community power study' (University of Reading, 1970)

Simons, M. 'Housing the Working Classes of Reading 1837–1939' (University of Reading, 2007)

Primary sources

Berkshire Record Office (BRO)

D/ECdT12/14: Papers from the Coley Park Estate

D/P 98 28/19, St Mary's vestry minutes, parish census

D/P 98 8/3 Vestry Minutes, July 1760

D/P 98 8/4 Vestry Minutes, Apr 1772

89/SCH/48/3 Coley School Log Books

Local Studies Centre, Reading Central Library

Reports of the Inspector of Nuisances; 1863–1865

Reports of the Medical Officer of Health for the Urban Sanitary Authority of Reading, 1880–1890

British Newspaper Archive

Extracts from the *Reading Mercury* (RM), *Reading Observer* (RO) and *Berkshire Chronicle* (BC)

Ancestry UK

St Mary's Census, 1841–1911

Electoral Registers

Parliamentary Papers Online

House of Commons: Report from the Committee on Silk Ribbon Weavers' Petitions, 3 June, 1818.

Online

https://berkshireresearch.wordpress.com/2014/04/18/berkshire-silk-weaving

Two Rivers Press has been publishing in and about Reading since 1994. Founded by the artist Peter Hay (1951–2003), the press continues to delight readers, local and further afield, with its varied list of individually designed, thought-provoking books.